High Hanging Fruit: A Proven Marketing Strategy For Ambitious Real Estate Agents

Tim Chermak
Copyright 2016

For Bella

Table of Contents

"Look at what the majority of people are doing, and do the exact opposite." –Earl Nightingale

Chapter One: The Most Expensive Marketing Mistake Made By Real Estate Agents (And How To Fix It Overnight)

Jose Medina will create over $250,000 of income this year as a real estate agent.

He doesn't drive a fancy car, live in a mansion, or work in a luxury market. His average transaction size is about $200,000.

Unlike the flashy brokers on real estate TV shows, Jose is a pretty normal guy. He doesn't list multi-million dollar properties. Or even million dollar properties. In fact, Jose rarely sells listings at *half* of that price point.

Last year, his most expensive sale was a $450,000 home. In his area, he considers that a high-end "luxury" listing.

His commission checks are not in the six figures, like the famous celebrity brokers you see on television.

Jose's average commission check is about $5,000.

Sometimes even less than that.

Jose cannot rely on closing just a few luxury listings per year. In his local market (Colorado Springs), most of the volume happens in the $150k-$300k range.

He is not selling Manhattan luxury penthouses for tens of million of dollars. Almost all of his listings are priced *under* $300,000.

Exceptions prove the rule.

Yet Jose Medina will create over $250,000 of income this year. That's over $20,000 *per month*, which is more than some real estate agents earn annually.

Jose earns a higher income than most doctors, lawyers, and business executives.

He plans to use some of that money to purchase investment properties and generate residual rental income. He'll be able to send his daughter to a private elementary school. He's considering buying a larger home for his family. Maybe a newer car.

Now that money isn't tight, the Medina family shops almost religiously at Whole Foods. Rather than the typical real estate agent diet of fast food drive thru meals and sugary energy drinks, Jose eats organic. He makes time to exercise every morning.

He's considering taking an entire month off next year, as a litmus test to see if his business can run successfully without him.

Jose is living "the dream" that attracts so many ambitious, hard working folks into the competitive game of residential real estate.

And because of his success, Jose's family is financially secure. In fact, by almost any reasonable standard, Jose is beyond financially "secure."

He is financially *wealthy*.

And he'll be the first to admit that his first $250,000 year *could have been much more*. He got overwhelmed with business during the summer, and intentionally slowed down his lead generation system so he could catch up with all the new prospects.

That's a good problem to have!

Jose's goal for next year is 100 transactions. He wants to create $500,000 of income for his family.

He's committed to that goal, and he knows it's possible. Especially considering he spent a lot of his time this past year showing homes to buyer clients. Some buyers looked at 10 homes before they decided to make an offer.

Jose knows this was probably an inefficient use of his time—getting to $500,000/year will require him to leverage himself. He will hire specialized buyer's agents to handle this in the future. It will be a difficult transition, because Jose loves working directly with clients (and seeing their faces when they close on their dream home).

But Jose is learning that it's not all about *him*. It's about delivering results for his clients with a predictable system.

Jose Medina does not trade hours for dollars. He doesn't think in linear terms. His mindset is exponential.

He is more than a real estate agent. Jose is a businessman.

He has stepped off the hamster wheel of the real estate rat race, and created a real *business.*

Why do some real estate agents struggle to earn $50,000 a year, while agents like Jose create over $250,000 a year of income?

The answer to this question might surprise you.

It's not a trick question, but it will probably challenge your assumptions.

It will make you think about your real estate business in an entirely different way.

The answer to this question is not complicated. The answer is not the latest FSBO direct mail campaign, a phone script for expired listings, or a killer Facebook ad template.

Those are all *tactics.*

The real answer isn't even a strategy (what comes before tactics). There are no "secrets" to reveal here.

If it were that easy, everyone would be selling 50+ homes a year. But they are not. Because it is *not* easy.

Did you know that most agents sell less than 10 homes per year? Many sell just four or five.

The difference between an "average" real estate agent's income and the income of a top producer is staggering. Some might even call it "unfair."

Now, of course, in the business world there is no such thing as "fair" and "unfair."

There is simply *reality.*

And the reality is that top producing agents like Jose don't have time to complain or make excuses.

They are focused on ONE THING.

It's the *one thing* that separates $250,000 earners from $50,000 earners. It's the difference between selling 50 homes a year and selling 10.

The answer to the question of why some agents earn 10x more than their peers goes beyond strategy.

It's about your *philosophy.*

It's about how you think about your business.

It's about understanding the inputs and outputs that create your income, and leveraging the most important input.

It's about becoming a master at one *specific* skill, and focusing the majority of your time and energy on that one skill.

That skill is MARKETING.

Specifically, a contrarian marketing approach called "picking the high hanging fruit."

It's the opposite of what most agents are taught. At first, it defies common sense. Why would you target the high hanging fruit when there's low hanging fruit that's easier to pick?

The answer is in the question: *because that's what everyone else is doing.*

Focusing on the high hanging fruit will require a ladder, some muscle, and a good dose of determination....but the results speak for themselves.

It is a revolutionary marketing approach for ambitious real estate agents.

Chapter Two: The Original Ad That Generated 97 Qualified Leads In Less Than Two Days

Debbie Caylor needed a miracle.

After two decades in the business, her real estate career was falling apart. The real estate crash of 2007-2008 devastated her monthly income, and there was no light at the end of the tunnel.

Debbie had no leads.

No upcoming closings.

No deals "in the pipeline."

Her business wasn't sick or dying...it was already dead and on life support.

Debbie was borrowing small amounts of money from friends and family, just to pay the bills every month.

She had started applying for "real jobs," but was having trouble finding anything available. She contacted local staffing services to look for local or regional sales positions.

No luck.

She even created profiles on the national job search websites, hoping to find *something* that would pay the bills. Anything to create some temporary cash flow, until her business picked back up.

But it didn't.

During the housing bubble, Debbie had been selling 40 homes a year. Like most other agents, she took the artificially hot market for granted. Debbie assumed it would always be this "easy" to make six figures in real estate.

She cruised to listing appointments and closings in a new car, and enjoyed the convenience of an expensive lakeside office suite.

Now, she was struggling to come up with enough money to buy toiletries.

Debbie quickly realized that she might have to give up real estate entirely, and find a new career.

And this wouldn't be easy—especially in the midst of a recession.

Debbie had spent the last two decades of her life building up a "book of business." She had devoted her career capital to the real estate profession. Her connections were in real estate. Her mentors were in real estate. Her skillset was in real estate.

Were the last twenty years of her life a sunk cost? Would she have to give it up, move on, and try out a new career?

As a real estate agent, Debbie's income completely depended on successful closings. And the number of closings depended on the number of leads coming into her sales funnel.

Which was exactly....zero.

She couldn't afford her mortgage payments, she needed a new vehicle, and to top it off, her team of agents slowly left her....one by one.

And looking back, she can't blame them. She wasn't sharing leads with them, because she didn't have any.

There was nothing to share!

Things hit rock bottom when Debbie realized her checking account was running so low, she didn't have money for toilet paper.

Because of financial troubles, she didn't have a credit card to rely on.

And this raises an interesting question: how do you grow a business when you don't have any cash to invest?

Generating leads costs money. A new website costs money. Billboards cost money. Newspaper ads cost money. Everything we typically associate with marketing...costs money!

It takes money to make money, right? Most small business owners, regardless of whether they work in real estate, believe this is true. Debbie Caylor thought this was true.

Until she found out it wasn't.

Debbie revived her career with a marketing strategy that didn't cost her any money—just her time.

And without any clients or prospects to work with, time was the only thing she had a surplus of.

During the housing boom of the mid 2000's, Debbie Caylor was very successful. She drove an Audi, and lived in a beautiful lake home.

Life was good.

But, as many agents discovered, it was an illusion.

The real estate bubble of the mid 2000's was a false prosperity. Like the *Great Gatsby* era of the Roaring Twenties economy, the housing market was completely unsustainable.

In some markets, neighborhood prices appreciated at 10% a year *or more.*

Economists disagree on whether the housing bubble caused a full-blown national depression. But that depends on who you ask!

As the saying goes, "When your neighbor loses his job, it's a recession. When you lose your job, it's a depression."

Debbie Caylor was in an economic *depression.*

But after 23 years in the business, she became an overnight success with one simple advertisement.

The ad was different from every other real estate advertisement in her market. She wasn't offering a free CMA, bragging about her production numbers, or posing with a set of keys–the typical content of agent advertising.

Rather than playing it safe, Debbie decided to try something radically different.

Something that would differentiate her from the competition.

Something that would position her as an expert authority.

Something that would actually *generate leads.*

Her experiment paid off...big time. The simple ad Debbie ran created almost 100 leads, and the business generated from that single advertisement tripled her income that year.

It actually created a huge problem for her—Debbie wasn't used to working with more than a dozen clients at a time. All of a sudden (*literally* overnight) she had 97 prospects to call, take notes on, and cultivate into buyers and sellers.

Debbie had no internal process to follow up with all of this new business, and her previous "system" of Post-It notes and calendar reminders wasn't enough to keep up with the avalanche of leads.

She quickly became overwhelmed with all of the new business, and had to hire an assistant to help her with all of the "behind the scenes" operations of the business.

That's a good problem to have.

But let's step back for a moment, and analyze Debbie's situation from the 10,000 foot perspective.

What did she do differently than most agents?

What specific part of her ad compelled ninety-seven people to sign up and request more information?

And perhaps the best question....*why* did Debbie experiment with this new advertisement, and take a risk on something she had never tried before? Wouldn't it have made more sense to do something conservative that wouldn't lose money?

Remember, Debbie was down to her last few dollars. In both a literal and figurative sense, she had nothing to lose.

And that was her greatest tactical advantage.

Debbie needed to create results, ASAP. She didn't have the luxury of time. She didn't have the resources to "farm" an area with consistent postcard mailings, or buy an annual billboard package to increase her "brand awareness."

She needed results *now*.

Not next week. Not next month. Today!

There are three reasons Debbie's ad created such immediate, overwhelming results. First, it was a new, unexpected kind of ad. It didn't resemble typical ads that the public *expects* to see from real estate agents.

Second, it promised something of value to the reader. It wasn't just a giant image of her logo, or a cheesy slogan. The ad promised a free book about local real estate. Now *that's* a compelling message!

Finally, because of what she was offering in the advertisement (a free book), she had a logical reason for requesting the contact information of prospects—she needed to know where to mail their free book!

Debbie's ad worked because it offered something people actually wanted. It's as simple as that. If you want people to respond to *your* advertising, give them a compelling reason to respond!

Most people understand that the best ads are emotionally powerful. What they forget is that they're simultaneously *logical.* The best ads make so much sense that it never even occurs to the prospect that he or she is being "marketed to."

Imagine what was going through the mind of potential prospects when they saw Debbie's ad: "Wow! A free book about buying and selling homes! That sounds amazing. Here's my address and contact information. Please mail me that book!"

It doesn't *feel like* marketing. Even though most prospects are hesitant to register at a real estate agent's website, it's not because they are scared of surrendering their contact information! They're simply hesitant about giving up their contact information *without getting any value in return.*

Prospects don't want to be taken advantage of, but they *are* willing to make a fair trade: their contact info for your expert information.

As Debbie learned, as long as you generate leads *by delivering value* to interested buyers and sellers, time is the best salesperson. Each individual's circumstances will determine their sales cycle. For some, it may be 6 months. For others, it may be 6 weeks. Regardless of their unique situation, when the time is right, they will trust you to guide them through their transaction.

If you pick the high hanging fruit at the top of the funnel—as Debbie did—your prospects won't even consider working with the competition. If you've cultivated trust, the decision has already been made: *you* are their real estate agent.

Debbie's ad reveals an important marketing truth for real estate professionals: it's usually much easier to invest your time and energy creating compelling offers than it is trying to overcome mediocre offers with aggressive sales scripts. If you actually give people something they want, they will gladly qualify themselves!

If you don't do the smart work of serving your clients, you'll have to do the hard work of selling them.

When it comes to creating successful lead generation advertising, the only question that matters is *what are you offering potential prospects in exchange for their contact information?*

The fastest way to create a flood of buyer and seller leads is to make an offer that's so irresistible, they gladly register with their contact information.

Zig Ziglar once said, "You can have everything in life you want, if you will just help enough other people get what they want."

Once you understand this, marketing becomes very simple.

This is the essence of picking the high hanging fruit: offer potential prospects valuable information *early in the sales cycle*, before other agents start to target them. This valuable information can be in the form of a book, a professional video series, an audio recording, a free home value analysis, a credit score training for buyers, etc. Use your imagination!

The most important thing is that your offer is valuable enough to convince potential prospects to give you their contact information early in the sales cycle, long before other agents start to advertise to them.

By the time they are ready to buy/sell, they will not be low hanging fruit for other agents, *because you already picked it!*

For Debbie, offering a free book generated 97 leads in just one day. This high hanging fruit generated hundreds of leads and referrals, resulting in a $100,00+ increase to her annual income.

Chapter Three: High Hanging Fruit

My grandparents own a small apple orchard.

Growing up in rural Minnesota, it was one of my favorite places to go. The property is about twenty minutes from the nearest town—far enough to feel secluded, but close enough to be convenient. It is heaven.

My grandpa bought the property back in the 1950's, when land sold for about $10/acre! Crazy.

On its north, west, and south sides, the apple orchard is surrounded by corn fields (I'm sure the farmers rotate their crops, but that's how I remember it). The east side borders a lake. And this is a *real* Minnesota lake, not an oversized–pond-pretending-to-be-a-lake. A private peninsula splits the orchard in two, only accessible by a narrow gravel road. The property is like a scene out of a Norman Rockwell painting.

To this day, I think it's one of the most beautiful places in the world. But as a kid, I didn't really notice. I just thought it was "cool" to tell my friends that my grandpa owned an apple orchard.

And, well, I still think it's cool to tell my friends that my grandpa owns an apple orchard! I mean, seriously, does *your* grandpa have an apple orchard? That's what I thought.

I remember bringing my grandpa's apple juice to school as a kid. It never failed to elicit a confused comment of "That doesn't look like apple juice!"

To be fair, it didn't look anything like what most people think of as apple juice. But it was. It wasn't *my* apple juice that was weird...it was their idea of apple juice that was weird! Mine was authentic. With apologies to Coke, this was the real thing.

My friends didn't know any better, but their "apple juice" was a yellow, pee-colored imposter! Or so I thought. Unlike the sugary drink dispensed at hotel continental breakfasts, my grandpa's apple juice was dark brown. It had no added chemicals.

"My grandpa owns an apple orchard with its own apple juice. It tastes better than your juice," I would say to classmates unfortunate enough to be drinking the typical juice boxes sold at grocery stores.

I probably sounded like a total jackass. Or, at least as much of a jackass as you can sound like at age seven. But it gave me a unique, personal understanding of the agricultural process. Namely, that real food comes from farms (not laboratories). And that the closer you get to the farm, the better it tastes!

I won't pretend I grew up on a farm—I didn't—but I remember picking apples with my family. Every fall, we'd hop in the car and drive to the orchard. Even though I wasn't exposed to the hard work of maintaining the orchard on a daily basis, this did teach me the basic truth that apples didn't come from grocery stores.

Grocery stores bought them from farmers!

To get the best tasting apples, you can't buy them at the store. That's too late. You need to move up the supply chain and get as close to the original source as possible. If you buy your apples at the retail level, a middleman is profiting from the transaction. You aren't getting the best deal.

I know this from experience. On the rare occasions when my mom would was unfortunate enough to have to take me grocery shopping, we *never* bought apple products. Ever. Why buy overpriced apples at the retail level when we could get them at the orchard?

The grocery store is where *everyone else* bought their apples, so of course they would be expensive! And usually bruised.

There was a quantitative, economic reason to get our apples right from the orchard, but there was also a qualitative one: the closer you got to the original source, the more vibrant the taste.

It was almost like a different food entirely. The apples from my grandpa's orchard were juicier. And the apple juice was simply...better. It just wasn't comparable to the sugary crap my classmates had. Not even close.

As I'm sitting here typing this, it's hard for me to put into words how different my grandpa's apple juice tastes from the typical big box retail brands. It's like a different drink entirely. The only comparison I can think of is day-old gas station coffee versus a hand poured cup from one of those weirdo hipster coffee bars in Portland (where the underemployed-but-happy barista treats each cup of coffee as if it were a work of modern art).

Have you ever had a cup of coffee like that?

Usually they cost five bucks, which is an absurd amount of money to pay for a cup of joe. But when you taste it, you understand why! It ruins you for all other cups of coffee.

Once you've had a coffee experience like this, even Starbucks seems reasonably priced.

The same was true of my grandpa's apple juice—once you tasted it, you wouldn't ever want to drink commercial apple juice again. The flavor is more vibrant, nuanced, and layered. In layman's terms, it is simply better.

I'm thankful that I grew up knowing what real apple juice was *supposed to* taste like. To this day, I refuse to poison my lips with the fake stuff! And by that I mean "any apple juice that doesn't come from my grandpa's orchard."

It's a lesson I'm glad I learned at a young age: quality takes more time (and sometimes more money), but it's worth it.

Let's say you're baking an apple pie. What do most people do first? *Drive to the grocery store.* C'mon, it's not like apples grow on trees!

At the grocery store, they compare the apples to each other, trying to select the best ones. Some apples are better than others. Some aren't yet ripe, some are too ripe. Some are bruised. This is a zero sum game: other shoppers are doing the exact same thing. There is a limited amount of good apples, and if you can't find any good ones, you're simply out of luck. The only way to improve your chances is to get to the store earlier—before the rest of the shoppers. If you're first in line, you will be able to select the very best apples.

Sometimes there are simply no good apples, because other shoppers got to them before you. *And there's nothing you can do about it.*

Sound familiar?

For years and years, real estate agents have battled each other for the "good leads." It was, and is, a zero sum game. At any given moment, there are only a limited number of buyers and sellers. Unlike other industries, you cannot create markets from scratch. Either people are buying homes or they're not. No amount of clever marketing can convince a family to move if they're happy in their current home and neighborhood. It's a waiting game—wait for people to make the decision to list their home, *and hope they think of you when that time comes.*

It's no different than buying your apples at the grocery store. Even if you went to the store everyday, it's still a game of random chance.

There is nothing you can do, and no amount of marketing dollars you can spend, that will change the fact that there is a limited number of so-called low hanging fruit. In the average real estate market, there are hundreds of agents at any given moment competing over the same finite number of leads.

To make matters worse, many agents are perfectly willing to pay full retail price for leads. They purchase leads from companies like Zillow, who mark up the true cost of the leads so they can make a profit. Buy low, sell high.

Not that there's anything wrong with making a profit! Just remember that in a zero-sum game, their profit is your loss. When you buy leads at the *retail level*, you are overpaying.

This is one reason why the real estate industry is so competitive: most agents are acquiring their leads from the same companies as their competitors, which gives those companies pricing power with monopoly-like characteristics.

The agents *need* the business, so they have almost zero leverage. They must pay full retail price for the leads. The only way to save money is by converting a higher percentage of these raw leads into actual closed business.

Naturally, some agents rise to the top of this battle. Some are better at converting—they have slick sales scripts and time blocked schedules devoted to cold-calling and follow up.

Some simply have massive marketing budgets; they can practically buy themselves market share. Top of mind awareness is prohibitively expensive, but it *is* for sale.

Where both of these strategies fail is that they accept the premise that *agents must buy their way to market share, paying full retail price along the way.*

I fundamentally, passionately disagree. There is a better way.

The battle for the low hanging fruit is not a battle you want to win. It is a low margin race to acquire market share. The fiercest competitors ignore profits, sustainability, and long-term competitive advantage. Like Wall Street investment bankers, all these agents think about is hitting their monthly and quarterly sales targets. The only way for them to do that is to focus on the low hanging fruit.

They do not care about building a long-term business. They are willing to outwork you to win the battle of low hanging fruit.

Let them.

Out-think them, and win the battle of the *high hanging fruit.*

It's time to change the game. It's time to fight on your own terms. You don't have to engage in the collective madness of buying overpriced leads—you can create your own leads.

Accessibility is a poor substitute for quality. Just because something is easy to get doesn't mean it's worth having! While other agents hunt for the next transaction, you can cultivate relationships.

Be a farmer, not a hunter.

While everyone else is fighting over the last apple on the low branch, you can set up a ladder. When everyone else abandons the tree to move on to the next one with some low hanging apples, you can climb your ladder and enjoy the high hanging fruit. You'll have it all to yourself: there is no competition at the top of the tree.

In real estate, there is no competition at the top of the sales cycle. Most agents spend all of their time and money competing in a zero-sum battle for the leads at the bottom of the funnel. By climbing the tree (moving up the funnel), you have access to the best apples. They are unmolested by other agents. They have not yet endured the humiliating sales scripts and hard sells at the bottom of the funnel.

At the top of the funnel, you have the time and social capital to invest in long-term relationships with your clients.

It's a better way of doing business. It's more effective *and* more efficient.

With no competition, the leads are cheaper. Instead of paying $30 or more per lead, you can create leads for as little as $5...or less.

At the bottom of the funnel, supply and demand work *against* you. At the top of the tree, the opposite is true: supply and demand is your friend. With minimal competition, the implicit "auction" system that determines the price of leads works in your favor.

The potential price of leads is always determined by the highest bidder. And if you're creating your own leads at the top of the funnel, *you are the only bidder.* It's automatically a buyer's market.

If you choose to target the high hanging fruit, a $500 budget can create as many as 100 leads. At the bottom of the funnel—where most agents foolishly pay full retail price for leads—that same amount of money may purchase as little as ten leads.

Is it more work to go after the high hanging fruit? Yes. Is it worth it? Absolutely. So have the courage to pick the high hanging fruit...*on private property, from trees that you own.*

As my grandpa taught me, the ultimate way to pick the high hanging fruit is to own your own orchard.

Chapter Four: A New Success Formula For The Future Of Real Estate

The year is 1994.

Bill Clinton is in the White House. Rush Limbaugh is a rising star in a new media format called "talk radio." The Rams still play their NFL games in Los Angeles. Pixar's first animated movie, *Toy Story*, won't be released for another year.

The world is a different place.

In 1994, the most popular movie of the year is *Forrest Gump*.

Americans still share common cultural experiences: they listen to the same music and watch the same TV channels as their neighbors. No one has hundreds of channels on their digital cable package, or access to thousands of movies on their Netflix account.

That's because digital cable doesn't yet exist. Neither does Netflix.

Buying books, a television set, or clothing at local stores is not yet a progressive idea. "Shopping local" is not the hipster concept it will soon become. It's simply what everyone does, because they have no other choice (Amazon.com quietly launches a year later, in 1995).

The Internet is about to change everything.

And nobody sees it coming.

As late as 1998, Nobel economist Paul Krugman infamously declares that, "The growth of the Internet will slow drastically. By 2005 or so, it will become clear that the

Internet's impact on the economy has been no greater than the fax machine's."

Like many others who failed to see the big picture, he was wrong.

Very wrong.

Throughout the 1990's and into the new millennium, the Internet changed every single industry on Earth. Some industries were affected less than others. Some were completely transformed.

The businesses that changed the most were those in and around the "information" industry.

Book publishers and media companies were the obvious "information" businesses. They had invested billions of dollars in the status quo, and the Internet threatened their entire business model. If people could quickly gain access to information online—often for *free*—how would they stay in business?

Does this ring a bell?

The real estate profession was no different. It took a cataclysmic event like the Internet to wake up the industry from its apathetic slumber.

(And, as I'll argue later in the book, most real estate agents still have not woken up from this dream. They are stuck in old ways of thinking.)

While it may be difficult to imagine, people didn't always have universal, instant access to customized information. The Internet is still a recent phenomenon.

When I speak at events, I often ask audiences to raise their hand if they used Google in the last 24 hours.

Nearly every hand goes up.

As a culture, we take the information revolution for granted. We forget that just twenty years ago, if you wanted to find answers to your questions, you had to get an encyclopedia! Or, if you were lucky, ask someone with relevant knowledge or experience. You couldn't just pull out your phone and Google something.

In fact, the previous sentence proves just how far we've come—I used Google as a *verb.* Oh, and you can access all of the world's information from your...phone.

Which is not only cordless, but now exists as a mobile device small enough to fit in your pocket.

Do you see where I'm going with this? *It's easy to take progress for granted.*

In the 1990's, Google was just a company. Not a verb.

Today, everyone knows what you're talking about when you "Google" something. You don't have to explain that you're going to use an online search engine called "Google" to access the world wide web. Furthermore, you don't have to explain what a "search engine" is!

Hmmmm, I don't know. I'll just Google it.

We nonchalantly use futuristic language that would have made no sense twenty years ago. We've come a long way!

The Internet has made the world a better place. What used to take hours now takes minutes. From an economic perspective, the productivity and efficiency gains have been staggering.

The "information revolution" fundamentally transformed the economy. Real estate was, and will continue to be, a big part of that transformation.

By recognizing the powerful *network effects* of the Internet (a fancy way of describing the profit potential of aggregating lots of people), companies like Google and Facebook have made billions of dollars.

Billions. With a "b."

That opportunity is still alive. Thanks to the Internet, real estate now offers a similar opportunity *at the local level.*

The first major disruption in the real estate industry occurred in 1994, when listing information was first published on the Internet.

Before the Internet, it was practically impossible to go house-hunting without a real estate agent. The only alternative would be driving around with a pen and paper, and writing down the address of every home you saw with a "for sale" sign.

Obviously, this would be very inefficient. So most people hired a licensed real estate agent.

Even if they would have preferred to go it alone, *they really had no choice.* There was no way to research the market or view the active listings without working with an agent. A licensed real estate agent was the only person with access to that information.

They were a means to an end.

Before 1994, real estate agents had a practical monopoly on information. Their power came from having access to data that buyers wanted. They were professional gatekeepers—guardians of "the book."

While commercial real estate has existed in one form or another for centuries, the modern real estate profession began in the early 20th century (brokerages began forming as far back as the 1850's, when *NP Dodge* and *Baird and Warner* officially opened their doors as America's first real estate brokerages).

The modern conception of a real estate agent can be traced to 1916, when the *National Association of Real Estate Agents* coined the now-trademarked term REALTOR®.

(I wonder if they originally pronounced it *real-tor?* Hmmm…)

From the start, real estate agents sought to brand themselves as professionals. At the time, being a "salesman" had a negative connotation. And it still does!

People looked down on salesmen as greedy, opportunistic hucksters who would say and do anything to make a quick buck. The Great Depression worsened this reputation, when millions of Americans lost their regular jobs and were forced into temporary sales gigs to pay the bills.

For many breadwinners, the only available jobs were 100% commission positions that created little risk for the "employer." The salesmen depended on their commission checks to feed their families, so they quickly learned the psychological basics of the manipulative *hard sell.*

When their wives and children relied on them for food and shelter, salesmen didn't have the luxury of building a relationship with their customers. They couldn't lengthen the sales cycle to cultivate more trust with their buyers. "Soft-selling" was a luxury they couldn't afford.

They needed to make sales, immediately.

Pop culture reinforced this stereotype with movies like *The Hucksters* (starring Clark Gable), and plays like Arthur Miller's *Death of a Salesman.*

Salesmen and advertising executives were shunned by more "dignified" professions like law and medicine.

Lester Wunderman, chairman of *Wunderman Cato Johnson,* and one of the greatest creative minds in the history of business, put it bluntly: "In those days, it was better to be a failed poet, a poor painter, or a philosopher-fool than to succeed in advertising—and perhaps it still is."

More recently, Alec Baldwin continued the tradition with his infamous "motivational" sales speech in *Glengarry Glen Ross.*

"Coffee is for closers!"

Obviously, Baldwin's character (a hot shot real estate executive who brags about driving "an $80,000 BMW") is an exaggerated caricature of ambitious agents.

His alpha personality doesn't care about anything (or anyone) unless it results in a closed sale.

Today, this reputation is alive and well.

And to be fair, it's not just real estate agents. Anyone who works in a sales industry has to overcome it—financial advisors, car salesmen, insurance agents, etc. Skepticism of salesmen is nothing new. The merchant classes of Rome and Greece dealt with the same branding problem.

And as long as real estate remains a "sales" business, it will always be this way. Potential buyers and sellers will always be skeptical of agents.

In a commission-based business model, the consumer is hyper aware of the incentives that motivate the agent.

This is true whether you're buying a house or a big screen TV at Best Buy. The context is largely irrelevant—human psychology is human psychology.

People will always be skeptical of salespeople.

The financial incentives of a commission-based business model create an agenda that isn't always aligned with what's in the best interest of the client.

But that's changing.

Throughout the twentieth century, working as a real estate agent meant you were a salesman...*who just happened to be working in the real estate industry.*

And this paradigm was (and is) the reason the public largely distrusted real estate agents. It had nothing to do with real estate—the skepticism was rooted in a generalized fear of salesmen.

Of course, the product being sold was much more expensive than the usual door-to-door deliverables like pots, pans, or encyclopedias....they were selling *houses.*

And because they were selling houses, the commission checks were considerably larger than those earned by their peers. You could sell a lot of encyclopedias and still not make as much money as the average agent earned off of one commission check.

Not surprisingly, when successful real estate agents began earning larger and larger incomes, skeptical homeowners started asking questions.

"How is he making so much money?!! *He's just a salesperson.*"

It's important to note that this historical skepticism towards agents had nothing to do with real estate. It had everything to do with their pre-existing prejudice towards the sales profession in general.

In their mind, a real estate agent was just a salesperson who happened to be selling houses instead of pots and pans.

Right or wrong, it is what it is.

For the most part, *the public was correct.* It wasn't just a "misunderstanding" or a branding problem.

Real estate agents were...and are...salespeople!

There's a reason the NAR invests so much resources in euphemistically presenting its members as *professional consultants*—they are trying to shed the old sales stereotype. They realized long ago that real estate agents did indeed have a branding problem.

However, as is true in other industries, branding is usually a *symptom*—not a cause. Branding victories (and defeats) are usually rooted in foundational truth.

And the most effective way to fix a branding problem is to address the underlying truth!

To succeed in the 21st century, real estate agents must evolve beyond their traditional role as salespeople. They are no longer hunters looking for a quick kill: they are farmers who intelligently cultivate their fields for steady and predictable returns.

The goal is no longer a quarterly sales target, it is creating and preserving *market share.*

The future of real estate will be more sophisticated, challenging, and calculated.

Less Hollywood, more Wall Street.

It's time for the real estate industry to embrace the business equivalent of moving from hunting to agriculture.

It's time to leave hunting behind, and reimagine an idea that's already popular in the real estate community: *farming.*

What would farming look like in our Information Age of ultimate Internet connectivity? What would farming look like when postage is "free" (email)?

Farming is the future.

Hard work will always be a tie-breaker, *but it can no longer be the sustainable competitive advantage it once was.*

In the past, a brand new agent could quickly achieve a 6-figure income if they were dedicated enough to make the necessary sales calls. Usually, this involved a tortuous schedule of cold-calling expired listings, FSBO's, and asking for referrals from the sacred sphere-of-influence.

Ask any top producer what got them to the top: *hustle* was the secret ingredient. If you worked hard enough, and put in long enough hours, you could make a surprising amount of money as a real estate agent.

In sales industries, the link between hard work and success is a virtual guarantee.

That being said, what happens when real estate is no longer about sales? What happens when *trust* becomes the new deliverable?

This changes everything.

Of course, hard work will never go out of style. It will always be necessary, but it's increasingly *insufficient.*

There are many agents who diligently put in the hours yet still struggle to make a dignified middle class income. No matter how many open houses they sit, no matter how many phone calls they make, they're chasing a moving target.

This trend will continue at an accelerating pace.

Hunting is simply too risky and inefficient once the competition has discovered the magic of farming.

The future of real estate belongs to intelligent planners who optimize marketing variables with controlled experiments, and manage their business like a farmer manages his fields.

More brains, less brawn.

Hunters rely on a mixture of hard work and luck. Farmers rely on advanced modeling, planning, and preparation. It's time for real estate agents to evolve from hunting to farming.

While other agents fight each other over the low hanging fruit at the bottom of the tree....bring a ladder.

Target the high hanging fruit.

It's time to transition from selling to *marketing.*

Chapter Five: Why You Should Stop *Selling* The American Dream (And Start Marketing It)

To be clear, there is nothing wrong with being a salesperson.

Sales are the lifeblood of the economy, and salespeople are the surgeons who keep it alive.

Without skilled, persistent, and persuasive salespeople, the brilliant ideas of our beloved scientists and engineers would never become reality.

As Jim Clifton says in *The Coming Jobs War*, "Innovation has little to no value until it joins with entrepreneurship."

Salespeople are just as necessary to innovation as the researchers in white lab coats.

In persuading someone to buy, a salesperson is literally selling them a better future. This may sound fluffy and esoteric, but the reason is actually quite simple: *before someone invests in a new reality, they must first believe that it's possible.*

In other words, they must be sold.

Whether the product is a whole-life insurance policy or the latest and greatest super HD television, the role of the salesperson is to convince the buyer *to convince themselves* that a better life is possible.

People hate to be sold, but they love to buy!

Good salespeople understand this psychology, and they use it everyday to make the world a better place.

It takes someone to convince the CEO to increase the R&D budget—that person is a salesperson. It takes someone to convince the public that the resulting product is interesting and valuable—that person is a salesperson.

If a tree falls in the forest and no one is around to hear it, does it make a sound? If a product is created and no one cares, does it exist?

Metaphysically, the answer is yes. Practically, the answer is a resounding *no.* A product that doesn't sell is no better than a solution that doesn't exist.

In fact, it's worse!

There is a very real cost associated with researching and developing products and services. If an equal amount of energy is not invested in marketing and selling the product....it is all for naught.

Product distribution is just as necessary as product creation. Which, of course, is a fancy way of saying that no matter how much our politicians talk about the importance of math, engineering, and science, it's ultimately *salespeople* that drive the economy forward.

For example, hundreds of millions of dollars are spent annually on finding a cure for cancer. And this is a great investment! Cancer is tragic. Horrific.

But it would be equally as tragic if a cure for cancer existed but wasn't selling.

Why? The end result is the same: people are deprived of a better life.

It is the salesman's job to create a better life for his customers by persuading them that it's possible.

Of course, the greatest salesmen are usually disguised by a different name: *entrepreneurs*.

At its core, entrepreneurship is about selling. It's about selling a unique vision that is so compelling it attracts investors….and creates billion dollar markets from scratch.

If Henry Ford hadn't sold the public on the benefits of his Model-T, we may still be riding horses. In fact, he admits that if he'd given people what they wanted, *he would have simply built a faster horse.*

Steve Jobs faced a similar sales challenge when Apple released the original iPod. Why would anyone want to carry thousands of songs around with them wherever they went?

Jobs was a master salesperson. He was uniquely skilled at selling people products that they didn't even realize they wanted. Apple now has more positive cash flow than the United States government.

We call this "entrepreneurship," but it's really just leveraged sales. Every entrepreneur, without exception, is a skilled salesperson. In fact, it's the essence of what it means to be an entrepreneur!

But the future of real estate will require a different set of skills.

What if traditional hard-sells (which are euphemistically described as "scripts") could be replaced by relationships?

What if sales was replaced by *marketing?*

For a long time, I've believed that the energy required to sell is inversely proportionate to the energy invested in marketing.

Think of a real estate transaction as a two-person relay race. The first leg is marketing. The second leg is sales.

Except there's an interesting twist: the two legs don't have to cover equal distances.

Marketing can run the first forty meters, and then pass the baton. Sales would run the final sixty meters. Or maybe marketing runs the first ten, and sales runs the final ninety.

This is a more accurate description of the current real estate status quo: marketing consumes 10% of the resources. Ninety percent of the energy is put into closing and converting leads...what we call *sales.*

What if we flipped this equation? What if marketing ran the first ninety meters, and sales was responsible for just ten percent of the so-called "sales cycle?"

In that case, it would be better described as a *marketing* cycle—not a sales cycle.

How would this change your mindset? This hypothetical scenario isn't just a thought experiment. It's the future of real estate.

Simply put, it's the difference between hunting and farming.

Hunting is stressful; farming is predictable.

When struggling real estate agents try to accelerate their income, they almost always look to sales strategies...not marketing strategies.

This is a mistake.

Almost automatically, hungry agents resort to cold-calling expired listings and FSBO's. They door-knock in target neighborhoods. They send desperate-sounding emails to their sphere of influence, begging for referrals.

In other words, they try to sell their way out of a marketing problem.

In almost every case, *they don't have a sales problem.* If they have no deals in the pipeline, it's not because they aren't converting leads. It's because they have no leads to convert.

The truth is, converting leads is not hard. In fact, it's incredibly easy! If you are failing to convert your leads, it's not a lack of sales skills—it's probably because you are trying to convert leads that just aren't ready.

The solution is simple: get them in your database months (or even years) before they're actually ready to buy a home.

If you provide real value—without being annoying—when the time comes for them to buy or sell, they will naturally choose you.

And the best part? It will be *effortless.*

Most agents try to "close" leads that just aren't ready yet. It's like trying to cut a frozen steak. It doesn't matter how sharp the knife—if the meat is still frozen, you won't make any progress.

The inverse is also true.

When an agent spends all their time at the bottom of the sales funnel, desperately trying to pick the low hanging fruit (expireds, FSBO's, and purchased Internet leads), it's the equivalent of eating a burnt steak. No matter how strong your sales skills—no matter how sharp the knife is—if the meat is already burnt to a crisp, it's simply too late.

No amount of seasoning, marinade, or steak sauce can reverse the reality of the situation. It's just too late!

Most agents try to compensate for their lack of marketing with aggressive sales hustle...and that is why they fail.

It's like trying to lose weight for your wedding by starving yourself for two weeks before the big day. Sure, you might see progress for a day or two, but it's ultimately unsustainable.

And more importantly, this is no way to live!

It would be much easier to take a long-term approach, make some basic lifestyle changes, and lose two pounds a week for a couple months.

The same is true of love and relationships (which has a lot more to do with sales psychology than you may think!).

If you want to find a committed lifelong partner, what do you think is the most effective way to find that person? There are really only two options: you could go to a bar and start asking strangers if they'd like to marry you...OR....you could cultivate meaningful relationships through the traditional dating process.

Which sounds better to you? Which would be more effective?

The former strategy depends on the law of large numbers: if you ask enough strangers, eventually someone will be dumb enough (or drunk enough) to say yes.

The latter depends on an entirely different approach: quality over quantity. By focusing on converting only warm leads, you drastically increase the likelihood of success.

Here's the kicker: *both techniques take the same amount of time and energy.*

That being said, which one makes more sense?

If I've learned anything about real estate marketing in the last couple years, it's that all the split-testing in the world cannot take the place of solid business fundamentals. You can experiment with all the headlines, ads, photos, and color schemes that you want—they are ultimately just details that have little to no effect on the big picture.

While micro-level optimizing is important (split-testing different ads against others), the real money is made at the macro level. Average real estate agents obsess over the latest and greatest marketing *tactics*, which seem to change every year.

Top producers operate on an entirely different level. They commit to executing a *strategy.*

This is as "80/20" as it gets: the decision to focus your energy on people *who actually want to hear from you* renders every other marketing decision unimportant.

In other words, stop trying to convert cold leads; start cultivating warm leads.

Spend your *money* at the top of the funnel (marketing), so you can spend your *time* at the bottom of the funnel (sales).

Invest your money implementing a consistent lead generation system so you can spend your time only talking with warm leads that are qualified, educated, and excited to do business with you.

It's really that simple.

You can do everything else in your real estate business completely wrong, and you will still experience success if you do this one thing right.

Remember the marriage metaphor? If the goal is simply to obtain sex as quickly and cheaply as possible, then there's nothing wrong with the aggressive approach. If you ask enough strangers for sex, the basic laws of probability will eventually work in your favor. At some point, someone will take you up on your offer!

It's inefficient, but if the goal is instant gratification (at the expense of long-term value), then it is technically effective.

The relevant question then becomes: would you rather be effective at real estate sales....or real estate *marketing?*

Chapter Six: The Terrifying Future Of Real Estate Marketing

Of course, it's a false choice.

You don't need to choose between effective sales and effective marketing. In the long-term, you can optimize both your sales *and* marketing strategies. But that's beside the point.

In the present (which is all that matters), most real estate agents chase short-term gratification at the expense of building a robust marketing system.

When it comes to investing your time and money, these are mutually exclusive choices. You can't be in two places at once, and you can't spend the same dollar on two different things.

What will you choose? Building a robust database, or chasing another angry FSBO? Will you do the *smart work* of using a ladder to pick the high hanging fruit? Or will you suffer through the hard work of fighting over the low hanging fruit?

Selling and marketing both require a commitment of financial and emotional resources. The difference is that marketing is scalable. You can cultivate the high hanging fruit with a budget of $500/month, a budget of $5,000/month, or a budget of $50,000/month. Marketing can scale with your business!

The low hanging fruit of sales is limited to the number of hours in a day. How many hours are you willing to spend cold calling? Suddenly, the "low hanging fruit" isn't as easy as it sounds.

The truth is, you can either have a transactional mindset or a relationship mindset. Either you are trying to *close* people or *cultivate* people. You can't focus on both at the same time. They are opposite and incompatible philosophies. The catch is that you will eventually create transactions (and referrals) using the relationship mindset.....but the inverse is not true.

Unfortunately, most real estate agents are addicted to picking the low hanging fruit. They are addicted to the immediate results. They don't have the patience to build a system with a steady pipeline of future business. It's no different from a chemical addiction to caffeine, sugar, or illegal drugs.

Making a conscious decision to start picking the high hanging fruit will be painful at first. It will require an intense (and sometimes painful) commitment to forming new habits. It's not just a change in the allocation of your marketing budget. It's an entirely new mindset.

As a real estate agent, it's easy to tell yourself that you have to spend your time doing what creates immediate results. You only get paid when you close a transaction! You don't get compensated for good intentions, right? If you have bills to pay and a family to feed, you can't afford to spend your time on long-term projects with a fuzzy ROI....right?

This makes intuitive sense. And that's why picking the low hanging fruit is such a dangerous addiction: it's easy to rationalize.

"I can't afford to spend money on building a pipeline of future business! In theory, it sounds great, but theory doesn't pay my bills. I need business now!"

The future of real estate promises a very different reality: you cannot afford *not to* cultivate a growing database of people.

As the real estate business model becomes more and more automated by technology (IDX is only the beginning), relationships will offer the ultimate hedge against uncertainty.

For example, what happens to real estate agents when virtual reality goes mainstream?

Don't kid yourself: Facebook is the world's leading technology company, and it's investing aggressively in virtual reality technology. In the next few years, you will be able to tour any home you want, without leaving yours.

Of course, this won't happen overnight. There will be speed bumps.

What will most likely happen is a forward thinking, disruptive real estate company will declare that: "technology is the future." They will make bold claims implying that real estate agents are irrelevant. And then the technology will flop. It will fail to produce results. Many blog articles will be written, keynote speeches given, and podcast rants published on "the preposterous idea" of real estate agents becoming irrelevant.

Those with a vested interest in the real estate industry (such as the NAR) will vigorously defend the sacred role of the licensed real estate professional.

"Technology can never replace local market knowledge and professional expertise," they will say.

And they will be right.

For a couple years, anyways.

It always takes disruptive technology a few years to transform the business model of an industry. Real estate will be no different. It will take a couple years—at the bare minimum—for this technology to catch on.

I wouldn't discount the likelihood of industry lobby groups using their political muscle to protect their members from "unfair competition." The NAR is politically powerful enough to pass legislation banning virtual reality—or anything that would threaten the livelihood of their dues-paying membership.

And it's not without precedent. This is what the taxi unions and hotel cartels did when Uber and Airbnb threatened their business models: instead of competing, they used political warfare to delay the inevitable.

But this won't change the reality that real estate agents need to evolve. Fighting technology is like fighting the tide.

It's a fight you will not, and ultimately cannot, win.

When virtual reality technology (and software in general) fails to completely eliminate the role of the real estate agent, it will be easy to say, "Look! Software can't replace an agent!"

Of course, this is a straw-man argument.

Few will claim that technology should completely replace the unique role of human beings in a real estate transaction. But the hours and hours of $20/hour work that goes into the typical real estate transaction can, and should, be as automated as possible.

From an economic perspective, this is a wonderful thing. It frees up more time for productive tasks that are worth $200/hour versus $20/hour.

With less time spent on low-value activities, professional agents will have more time to spend on strategic thinking and implementation.

Are you ready for a world where you're expected to contribute at the $200/hour level?

The truth is that many agents are not prepared for this shift. They like to kill time on mindless tasks like MLS data entry, rearranging their CRM, and typing half-assed blog posts that no one reads.

Obviously, everyone knows that real estate isn't an hourly position with weekly W-2 paychecks. It's an entrepreneurial opportunity with big risks and big rewards.

This isn't a secret—it's the very reason most agents got into the business in the first place!

But for most agents, this is just *theory*...not wisdom.

In a world where $20/hour work consumes much of the average agent's time, it's easy to average out the hours into an aggregate.

Because they earn roughly X dollars per year, they subconsciously assume that their time must be worth around X per hour. It's easy to assume that all hours are created equal. It's easy to assume that you're getting paid for "putting in the time."

It's easy to depend on linear assumptions in an exponential world.

Of course, you know what they say about assumptions...

The truth is that most agents earn 95% of their income from about 5% of their time. That five percent is spent doing incredibly leveraged, strategic marketing work.

Are you ready to compete with agents who understand this not only theoretically, *but practically?*

As Jim Rohn said, "You don't get paid for the hours you work, you get paid for the value you bring to those hours."

Not all hours are created equal.

This is why two agents in the same market could both work a standard forty-hour week, and make completely different incomes. Agent A might earn $150,000 a year, while Agent B earns $60,000 working *the same amount of hours in the same market at the same brokerage.*

Clearly, "putting in time" is a completely irrelevant, insignificant, and ultimately useless way to measure productivity in your real estate career.

No one—especially your clients—cares about how many hours you're working. What they care about is how much value you're creating for them. If you create more value, you'll get paid more!

I know that for many readers, this may not be breaking news. You may already be a successful agent earning $250k+ that knows how to leverage time. Or maybe you're earning less than half of that, but you're committed to taking your career to the next level.

No matter where you fall on the income scale, you need to prepare for a more efficient future. The future of real estate will not tolerate being "busy" with low value activities.

As Tim Ferriss says, "Being busy is a form of laziness. Lazy thinking and indiscriminate action."

If I could narrow it down to one phrase, the future of real estate can be described by the Orwellian cliché *less is more.*

More will be accomplished by fewer agents.

Here's a bold prediction: in the next ten years, there will be far less full-time agents than there are today. However, the agents that evolve with the times will not just survive, they will thrive. With less competition, they will consolidate their local competition into functional monopolies.

Instead of ten agents in a small town earning $50,000 a year, it will probably be two agents earning a quarter million apiece. The total transaction volume will stay the same, but it will no longer be split up amongst ten agents.

The most productive, efficient agents will create powerful local brands that protect their monopoly status. For them, the coming technology revolution will be a windfall opportunity.

With less competition, there will be higher margins, and therefore greater incentives for true *client service.*

Economically, nothing will affect the demand curve of homes themselves. That's beyond the scope of this book. The relevant changes will be in the demand for the traditional services of a real estate agent.

Less is more.

Look at how technology has already influenced traditional sales and service professionals like travel agents or financial advisors. The business models of these industries are very similar to real estate. Their transformation provides extremely relevant case studies for how real estate may evolve.

It's not that travel agents or financial advisors are extinct—nor are they even an endangered species. They have simply evolved to match the realities of the modern consumer: there are no longer an abundance of poorly trained stock brokers with cheap strip mall offices selling in-house, proprietary mutual funds—this type of "investing" can be easily automated online, saving the average retail investor thousands of dollars in fees.

It's a victory for the investment brokerage—they get to eliminate the costly middleman, and therefore free up countless resources for more marketing promotion of their products. It's also a victory for the consumer: they save thousands of dollars on inefficient fees.

The only loser is the middleman who didn't see it coming.

Travel agencies tell a similar story. Booking a vacation used to involve calling your local travel agent, and letting them handle all of the details. Since they possessed a practical monopoly on information, their services were always in demand as long as people were taking vacations. The only external threat to their business was an economic recession, but that was not a problem unique to the travel industry. When people had to use your services to take a vacation, it seemed like a lucrative business to be in!

Until it wasn't.

Sound familiar?

Travel agents and financial advisors used to share the same positioning as real estate agents: their primary deliverable was access to information. They directly profited from information asymmetry: they knew something that the consumer didn't, and they made a living by selling that information and expertise.

When the information became freely accessible, all they had left to sell was their expertise. And it turns out that most people aren't willing to pay exorbitant fees for highly subjective travel or investment advice.

Most people...but not *all* people.

Both of these industries have since pivoted their business models. They now target higher-margin, affluent clientele. They make the same amount of money working with fewer clients.

Less is more.

While there are still hard working travel agents who broker reasonably priced vacations (and financial advisors whose primary clientele are middle class retail investors), the vast majority of them have repositioned themselves as a luxury service for the affluent.

Software now does the job that they used to earn a living on, and so they've repositioned their brands as luxury alternatives. For those who want custom solutions to highly specific needs, there are still travel agents and financial advisors.

And they're more profitable than ever.

This same process has played out in other industries, too. For centuries, horses were the standard mode of transportation. Today, cars are how the average person gets from point A to point B. Horses are now a luxury good owned by mostly rich people who can afford the costs.

The cruise ship industry followed a similar path—world travel used to be on ships. Today, it is much, much cheaper to fly. In fact, a first class ticket is often cheaper than a comparable cruise to the same location. Cruise ships are simply less efficient, so they repositioned themselves as a high margin luxury good.

They realized they could no longer compete in the transportation business, so they decided to keep the assets but change the marketing. They're now in the *vacation* business.

See the difference?

Real estate agents will need to make a similar transition. No longer will they be in the "drive clients around town to look at houses" business, or the "send me a report of active listings that fit my criteria and price range" business.

Both of these can be automated.

Even buyer showings, which most people assume require an agent's physical presence, could easily be conducted without a licensed agent.

Imagine a system where a buyer first meets with a licensed agent (in person) to discuss their real estate needs. To minimize any potential risk of burglary/property damage to the seller, the agent verifies that they are in fact a "legit" homebuyer. This verification process could include a credit check, background check, personal/professional references, etc.

Once the agent has given them the official verification (which may even include a lender pre-qualification), they would receive their own personalized access code to unlock any lockbox in their local MLS association.

The future of house hunting doesn't require real estate agents. And it shouldn't!

Why should buyers pay thousands of dollars in indirect commissions (reflected in the higher sales prices necessary to pay out the buyer's agent split) when the bulk of the agent's time is spent "showing homes?"

Which, of course, is a clever euphemism for unlocking doors. I assure you that if someone qualifies for a mortgage, they are probably more than capable of unlocking a door.

It's simply not worth paying 3% of the home's purchase price to someone who professionally opens doors and fills out paperwork. It's not that this work is unnecessary, *it's that most buyers would prefer to do it themselves and pocket the difference.*

It is inefficient.

There's a reason a "buyer's agent" is seen as the low rung on the corporate ladder of a real estate brokerage. The next step is to eliminate the position entirely—that's my prediction.

A far better solution would be for buyers to directly absorb the costs of working with a dedicated buyer's agent.

This may take the form of a flat fee, or perhaps a hybrid model combining a flat fee plus an hourly charge. The specifics don't matter. The point is that markets always move towards efficiency, and real estate is no different.

Remember: if the only obstacle for innovation is an artificial barrier to competition (like association rules or political legislation created by lobbyists), innovators will eventually innovate a way around the rules.

Disruptive companies like Uber and Airbnb rocketed to billion dollar valuations not because of a cool product, but a new *platform*. The platform unlocked billions of dollars of value that was being held hostage by an inefficient business model.

I predict the same thing will happen to the real estate world.

As I've said before, the specifics are irrelevant....all that matters is that free markets do not tolerate inefficiency. Real estate is not immune from the basic laws of economics.

For many phases of the transaction, real estate agents are nothing more than a middleman. And as technology continues to improve at an accelerating pace, the traditional role of being a "market maker" is increasingly obsolete.

The middleman is about to be cut out.

Fewer agents will do more of the deals.

Because future technology will streamline transactions, it will become increasingly difficult to survive as a real estate agent if you aren't spending your time on high-level, strategic objectives.

And here's the most important part of all this: the aforementioned technology *probably hasn't even been invented yet.*

Earlier I mentioned the potential of virtual reality, but it may be something entirely different. I can't predict the specifics, but I can predict that technology will eventually automate everything that can be automated.

It's not a matter of if, but when.

And this brings up an important question that all real estate agents should ponder: what *cannot* be automated?

In the real estate industry, there are relatively few activities that fit this criteria. They are almost always related to client acquisition and retention—what the corporate world describes as "business development."

(For a crash course on the importance of strategic time management—especially as it relates to the future of real estate marketing—I highly recommend you check out the book *80/20 Sales And Marketing* by Perry Marshall. Perry is not a real estate agent, but he's a damn good marketer— one of the best in the world. And his ideas about business growth as it relates to the individual entrepreneur are priceless. You can pick up a copy of this book for less than twenty bucks, but it's worth at least ten times that!)

Ultimately, there is only one protection that I know of that makes technology irrelevant. It's the only thing that software cannot make obsolete. When the day comes that disruptive real companies attempt to "cut out the middleman" (it's coming sooner than you think), there will only be one effective defense.

Rather than fighting a war of efficiency, smart agents will live to die another day. They will play another game entirely. They will compete with *effectiveness.*

Instead of fighting over the low hanging fruit, they will stand on a ladder and pick the high hanging fruit. They will generate, cultivate, and convert their own leads. They won't be dependent on outside companies selling them leads. They will own their own orchards, and strategically pick the high hanging fruit.

Just like a local brick n mortar retailer that attempts to out-discount Wal-Mart, real estate agents will not be able to fight the future. It's a race to the bottom. The only possible outcome is discounting commissions to the point that they're working for minimum wage against technology that is willing to work for free (and doesn't require a benefits package with dental coverage).

Are you ready to compete in a market that thinks real estate agents are as irrelevant as travel agents? This brave new world is not a hypothetical, dystopian future.

It *will* happen in the next ten years.

When the rules of the game make it impossible to compete, the ultimate survival strategy is playing by a new set of rules.

Fight on your own terms. Change the game.

For ambitious real estate agents, the solution is simple. Not easy, but simple: the one thing technology cannot replace is a *relationship.*

When you cultivate quality relationships with your prospects, you don't need to resort to "quantity" tactics. It's better both financially and emotionally to convert a high percentage of warm leads than a low percentage of cold leads.

Ask yourself: would you rather convert four out of a hundred, or four out of ten?

Both scenarios create four commission checks. However, it doesn't take a genius to figure out that converting four out of ten leads is vastly preferable to four out of every hundred.

Psychologically, it's night and day.

This is the proper role of marketing!

It makes sense *financially*: higher conversion percentage and therefore a more efficient cost-per-lead.

It also makes sense *emotionally*: more time spent working with quality leads versus stressful cold calls with hostile strangers.

For most real estate agents, this is a completely new approach. A paradigm shift. It involves building a list of buyers and sellers, knowing from the start that the sales cycle could be months or even years, and cultivating them accordingly.

It's thinking like a media company: build an audience, build trust with that audience, and monetize the long-term relationship.

Of course, this is the opposite of what most real estate agents have done, are doing, and will do.

And that's why it's such a compelling opportunity for those who see the future of real estate.

Let's go back to the future.

In the pre-Internet days, building a business was about building your database. Period. It was really that simple!

The more relationships you had, the more homes you would sell. The entire goal of marketing was to have "mindshare" with your sphere of influence.

Before online companies like Zillow or Trulia came along, people had to call a real estate agent to start the house hunting process. There was simply no other option. You couldn't begin your home search on the Internet, and then contact an agent only when you had already found some potential properties online.

To even get the process *started*, you first had to contact a real estate agent.

In this environment, marketing was simplified. You didn't need to buy zip codes from Zillow, or invest in expensive pay-per-click ads on Google. You didn't need to worry about optimizing your website for SEO. All that was required was to stay *top of mind* with your sphere of influence.

That's it. Nothing more, nothing less.

When someone decided to sell their home, you wanted them to immediately think of you!

To achieve this, agents did anything and everything to get noticed. They mailed recipe cards for chocolate chip cookies (branded with their logo, of course). They sent birthday cards to their clients. They called them a couple times a year "just to check in." They hosted annual client appreciation events, with catered food and wine.

Famous sales trainer Tom Hopkins personally delivered pumpkins, door-to-door, in affluent neighborhoods he wanted to "farm."

Of course, most of these tactics were really cheesy. But guess what—they worked!

It was the same tactics being used in other industries like insurance or car sales. In a world without the Internet, *the best marketing was a relationship.*

And it still is.

Chapter Seven: Why The Internet Is A Real Estate Agent's Best Friend

Before the Internet, a real estate agent was little more than a librarian with sales skills: clients told them what they wanted, and the agent consulted "the book" to find a match.

In the 1960's, early beta versions of what is now the *Multiple Listing Service* were launched. For the first time ever, brokers could consult "the book" to sell all of the market's current inventory—not just their own listings.

(While today it's often a distinction without a difference, this was the original difference between an agent and a broker: a broker could *broker* agreements between different agencies instead of just selling their own listings.)

The book was usually updated on a weekly basis with active, pending, and sold listings. Short of burglarizing a real estate office in the middle of the night, the only way to get access to the all-important book was to schedule an appointment with a licensed agent.

In this sales environment, the deliverable was not service, market knowledge, or negotiating skill. The real estate agent was simply selling *access.*

When a prospect wanted to start house-hunting, the first step was to contact a real estate agent. There was no way around it. No other options. No other alternatives. If they were serious about buying a home, the prospect had to schedule an appointment with a licensed real estate agent.

Period. End of story.

There was no online database of listings, because, well, the Internet didn't exist.

Ah....those were the good old days!

Of course, this was wildly inefficient.

There was no logical reason that real estate agents needed to guard "the book." As technology futurists have been saying for decades, *information wants to be free.*

This doesn't mean books, movies, and other forms of information should cost zero dollars; it means that universal access to information should not be restricted by artificial barriers.

In other words, real estate agents should rely on professional expertise as their job security, not on restricting access to the MLS. Those days are long gone.

Information wants to be free.

Like it or not, this is a core belief of the millennial generation—which has now surpassed the baby boomers as the largest generation in American history.

And it's not just youthful idealism: information freedom is rooted in basic economics. It's increasingly unprofitable to make money by selling access to information.

Someone will always be willing to give it away for free. It's the ultimate price war (not a war you want to win)!

Any business model that is dependent on an artificial restriction of information will be wiped out by innovative competition that gives away the information for free *and finds other ways to monetize the demand.*

The most obvious example is Zillow. Zillow's core product is simply access. They are giving away for free what used to be a licensed privilege: access to current market inventory. Instead of charging consumers for access to their database, Zillow created a sustainable business model that ensured the information would remain free to consumers: they charge agents to access the consumers.

If you think about it, this represents a complete reversal of the prior model. Instead of consumers paying a price to access the information, it is now real estate agents who are literally paying to access the buyers.

As Chris Anderson wrote in his controversial book *Free*, "In a competitive market, price falls to the marginal cost."

Since it didn't cost agents anything to access the available inventory, it was only a matter of time before this artificial barrier was eliminated.

It's difficult to charge people for something when they know you are getting it for free! The real estate industry can no longer sell access. It has to move up the value chain and start selling *expertise.*

And if it's true that information wants to be free, it's equally true that wisdom wants a premium price. If history is any indication, people are happy to pay for professional wisdom.

Because it's no longer profitable to sell or otherwise restrict information, it's often used as "bait" to sell other products or services. Hook consumers with free information, and then sell them something that actually makes money!

In my opinion, this marketing reality is not yet understood by most real estate agents. And that's a huge opportunity for you, dear reader.

65

Coffee shops use free wifi to sell a ten-cent cup of coffee for three dollars. Movie theaters hope to break even on their ticket sales so they can sell high-margin concessions like popcorn. Keep in mind that "entertainment" is merely *information* that's enjoyable.

In our millenial-dominated world that demands everything be "free," it's easy to forget that public wifi access used to cost money! Most places charged by the hour. Sometimes you even paid in fifteen-minute increments!

Craziness.

Today, this seems ludicrous. Wifi is offered for free basically everywhere! It's no longer a competitive advantage...*everyone* has free wifi.

Think about it. When was the last time you went to a coffee shop that *didn't* have free wifi?

And it's not just coffee shops.

I sometimes laugh when I see businesses advertising "free wifi," as if it's somehow a unique offering. Everything from restaurants to movie theaters to gas stations has free wifi. These days, you *expect* public businesses to have a free wifi signal for their guests.

Imagine if a coffee shop attempted to charge you $5/hour for wifi. There would be a public outcry! Maybe even a boycott. People expect wifi to be freely accessible.

Call it entitlement, call it whatever you want. In our modern "information economy," consumers demand uninterrupted access to information.

Why would real estate information be any different?

Restricting information on active listings is a losing strategy. That's why IDX feeds have exploded in recent years.

It's no longer a "cool feature" to have an IDX feed built in on your website. It's required. It's table stakes. In a world where consumers are used to having *instant access* to whatever they damn well please, you must give it to them.

The customer isn't always right, but they *are* the boss.

When the Internet transformed the real estate industry, it didn't really transform anything except people's mindsets and expectations. People still buy and sell homes the same way.

It didn't change the agent's day-to-day responsibilities (other than the necessity of learning how to navigate MLS software).

Instant access to information illuminates a foundational truth about real estate marketing: the real value provided by a licensed agent was never about access to the MLS.

And it never will be.

The real value is knowing the market inside out. It's being able to give advice on different neighborhoods, listing price strategies, marketing techniques, and house hunting timelines.

It's knowing the right lender to recommend, the most reliable plumber, or the most thorough home inspector. The real value is in being a true real estate *consultant.*

Which can be summed up in one word: trust.

People work with consultants for one reason, and only one reason: they trust them to produce results.

If this were not the case, no one would hire a consultant! They would do it themselves.

In real estate, the most obvious example is the infamous "For Sale By Owner" listing, whose hideous black and orange yard signs are an ever-present reminder to real estate agents that trust is the real product being bought and sold.

Homebuyers no longer need real estate agents to show them what's currently available. You can complain about it, you can wish things would go back to the way they used to be, but *it is what it is.*

Access to information is not a product people are willing to pay for. And this is not surprising: in and of itself, data is useless. Knowing how many listings are active in a certain zip code is not enough to make an informed buying decision. Even more "advanced" metrics like price per square foot don't tell the whole story.

Raw information requires a skilled interpreter to become useful. The value is in the application, not the possession, of information.

And in the interpretation industry, business is booming. Wisdom never goes out of style.

Chapter Eight: Will Real Estate Agents Become An Endangered Species?

Will the Internet make real estate agents irrelevant?

It's certainly not without precedent—I've written elsewhere about travel agents and financial advisors, who are struggling to reinvent themselves after being blindsided by digital disruption. A similar fate fell upon business models like video rental, where the core deliverable wasn't the actual movies, but aggregation and access to movies.

The lesson is clear: never confuse your deliverable with the real business you're in.

If travel agents had realized they were in the vacation business, not the travel-booking-middleman business, they could have leveraged the Internet as an *opportunity* rather than a threat. Instead, they were all but wiped out when booking vacations became as simple as logging onto the Internet in the comfort of your own home. The complex algorithms of travel-booking websites find the cheapest flights and hotel rooms for you…for free.

All of a sudden, working with a travel agent is more of a hassle than just doing it yourself.

Could this happen to real estate agents?

It's not an isolated incident. When companies mistake their present deliverable for what business they're *really in*, they are vulnerable to the first competitor who identifies the resulting asymmetry.

Netflix brutally murdered traditional video rental companies like Blockbuster, *but the movies didn't change.* This is an important truth that is easily missed. The innovation wasn't in the product, it was in the business model itself.

Consumers are still buying movies, they're just buying them differently.

In the same way, Americans are still buying homes. They're just buying them differently.

No one drives to a Blockbuster to rent a movie anymore, and no one meets with a real estate agent to buy a home, either. At least, that's not how the process *starts.*

By the time they decide it's time to contact a licensed real estate agent, most homebuyers have already spent hours and hours searching for homes online. Not to mention the hundreds of hours they probably spent watching *House Hunters* on HGTV, being indoctrinated with dramatized half-truths and unrealistic expectations about the buying process.

Like it or not, this initial research does not require a real estate agent.

If the buyer could avoid scheduling a meeting with a licensed agent, they would. While it may be uncomfortable to hear, the agent is little more than a *necessary evil* from the perspective of the client.

If they could buy or sell a home without you, they would. And, as we all know, every year many of them try (and usually fail). FSBO signs are a reminder of this inconvenient truth.

In this sense, technology hasn't changed the motivations of buyers and sellers. It has simply revealed the preferences they had all along. It's not as if they were excited to work with agents before the Internet!

Today, they aren't forced into meeting with a licensed agent. They can peruse listings for months before finally deciding to contact an agent. *They* are in control. They decide when it's time to officially start house-hunting. They decide when it's time to list their home for sale. They are in control, not you.

And that means agents have to *earn* the business.

Prospective buyers have never needed an agent to hold their hand while they page through listings. And they still don't!

Whether it was pages in "the book" or digital pages on a website, prospects would prefer to browse alone.

If you disagree, try the following: the next time a buyer lead contacts you, ask them if they'd like you to email a link with listings in their price range, or if they'd prefer you to print them off and meet you at your office.

Nine times out of ten, they will request the digital link. Maybe even ten times out of ten.

No one wants to meet with a professional salesperson until they absolutely have to (in case you forgot, that's what a real estate agent is: *a professional salesperson*).

Restricting access to the official database of listings (which at the time was a physical book) was little more than a job-security program for real estate agents. It sounds harsh, but it's true.

Similar to how modern ride-share companies like Uber are battling the taxi unions, real estate agents had an obvious vested interest in protecting their livelihood.

Restricting access to *the book* was one way of doing that.

But, like all artificial barriers to competition, it was little more than a speed bump. When the Internet burst onto the scene in the mid-nineties, prospects quickly realized that they didn't need a real estate agent *at this stage of the sales process.*

Key phrase: at this stage of the sales process.

Obviously, this was pretty awesome for the real estate industry! Imagine if you sold TV's, and the only way to research TV's was to come in to your retail store. It would be a compelling advantage...and it would be easy to sell a lot of television sets!

Of course, this was not a hypothetical. It was reality for TV salespeople (as well as other industries) before the Internet.

As most retail storeowners will attest to, 90% of the sales process is simply getting the customer in the door. Once they're physically in your business, you can build rapport. You can ask qualifying questions, and get to know the prospect's real needs. In short, once you meet a customer face-to-face, you can *cultivate a relationship.*

From the customer's perspective, a relationship usually trumps everything else. All things being equal, they will buy from whomever they trust. Especially on a transaction that's hundreds of thousands of dollars!

Trust is worth a lot of money.

Because most people won't (and shouldn't) trust a software algorithm to make financial decisions for them, it's highly unlikely that real estate agents will disappear.

Information can be automated; wisdom cannot.

When most people think about the future, they tend to dwell on its ambiguity, its vagueness, and its uncertainty. Fortunately, what *is* certain is the future demand for housing. This will require experienced and professional real estate agents!

Clients will continue to demand expertise and advice when buying and selling real estate. Some parts of this process *can, should, and will* be automated by technology. The real estate agent of the future will bridge this gap between raw information, curated knowledge, and experiential wisdom.

Here's the bottom line: technology can improve, *but not replace*, the special role of the real estate agent.

Nothing can change the fact that buying and selling real estate is a personal process. As long as humans are involved, it can never be reduced to a simple mathematical calculation. Choosing a home (or selling one) is much more emotionally complex than a software algorithm.

There is no shortcut here. Emotions and personal preferences affect the decision to buy a home. Managing this complex emotional process requires empathy and creativity: two characteristics in which humans have a decisive advantage over computers.

Most real estate agents *intuitively* understand this process. The soft skills that separate top producers from average salespeople are easy to identify, but hard to codify.

Some people call it emotional intelligence, some people simply call it "being good at sales."

How can some agents convert ten percent of cold leads, while the rest of the office struggles to convert less than half of that?

Could a computer program be a better salesman than an experienced real estate professional? Doubtful.

It doesn't matter if you're selling cars, appliances, clothing, or residential real estate: experienced salespeople understand the importance of getting face time with their customers. In fact, numerous studies show that a homebuyer or seller will work with the first agent they meet *in-person.*

Technology like the Internet changed that.

Or did it?

Chapter Nine: The Best Marketing Is A Relationship

Real estate used to be about buying expensive branding ads. You would invest thousands of dollars a year to "get your name out there." Some agents used highway billboards, some agents used print newspaper ads, and some agents targeted a "farm" area with regular mailers. The tactics were different, but the strategy remained the same: stay top of mind with your target market, so when the time was right they would call YOU and not the competition.

The calculation was simple: who they called was a direct function of who they trusted.

It was a *relationship* business.

It was a lot easier to keep existing clients than to generate new leads. It was a lot easier to ask for referrals than to reach out to complete strangers.

And it still is.

This era was defined by sales trainers like Tom Hopkins, who infamously went door-to-door in his target neighborhoods offering free pumpkins.

Hey, whatever works!

With the advent of the Internet, real estate evolved into a transactional business model. Instead of cultivating relationships, agents cultivated *transactions*. This is still the dominant mindset today.

At industry events or networking get-togethers, no one asks, "So, how many relationships have you developed this year? What's your goal?" A question like that would elicit a deer-in-the-headlights look from most agents. They do not measure their business in terms of relationships, or the resulting lagging indicator: referrals.

Agents think of referrals and relationships as "nice to have," almost like an added bonus. It's the icing on the cake. The real metric they care about is sales volume and number of transactions. Their identity is linked to their level of *production.*

"I did $6.2 million last year in volume," or "My goal is 50 transactions." Language is incredibly powerful! The words that most agents use reveal how they think about their business.

What gets measured gets managed.

Of course, it's a good thing to set sales goals! But the Internet has tricked many agents into compromising long-term security for short-term sales.

When agents block off time to call, they are not calling past clients to check in. They are using advanced dialers with software services that streamline the cold-calling process. Their goal is not to cultivate relationships, it's to cold-call as many expired's and FSBO's as possible.

They want to create as many transactions as they can, and cold-calling is a proven way of doing that!

It's inefficient, humiliating, perhaps even dehumanizing...*but it works.* And that's why it's a multi-million dollar industry. There are entire businesses devoted to this one tactic—many agents gladly pay $1,000+ every month for motivational coaching calls. There is not much substance to most of these "coaching" programs, other than providing accountability and motivation to keep making the necessary number of calls.

In my humble opinion, if you have to pay thousands of dollars a year just to "stay motivated," you're probably doing something wrong. Or, at the very least, you're using a very inefficient approach to accomplish your goal!

The proof is in how most real estate agents perceive the *opportunity cost* of their time: they will risk alienating a future client with aggressive sales scripts aimed at converting the low-hanging fruit. That is a tradeoff they are happy to make.

But the opposite is not true: they would never risk delaying a potential "conversion" by using a softer, more nuanced approach to cultivation. If they can't qualify the prospect and schedule an appointment in one focused call, they will quickly move on to the next lead.

From a finance perspective, they discount the value of future dollars to near zero.

When you operate with this implicit transaction mindset, time spent on cultivating long-term relationships is time that is wasted. This time could have been spent calling and converting prospects that are *ready to buy now*. While most agents would not be this blunt in describing their mindset, it is what it is.

Like doctors, lawyers, and other professionals with specific skillsets, the most valuable commodity a real estate agent has is time. Especially for agents who are already successful, how they spend their actual advertising dollars is less consequential than how they spend their time.

Whether explicitly or implicitly, every agent has a time budget for organizing their hours. How they allocate that finite budget reveals their priorities. It's a zero-sum game. Time is the ultimate non-renewable resource; once you spend it, it's gone forever.

Are you cultivating relationships or chasing transactions? Be honest.

There's no denying that the transactional approach works. While not terribly efficient, it is certainly effective. But it might not be *sustainable.*

As the business model of real estate continues to evolve, the first casualties of automation technology will be at the "bottom of the funnel." Companies like Zillow are already proving this, but the trend will accelerate in the coming years.

As a general rule of thumb, the best way to stay ahead of the curve (in any industry) is to ask yourself: what part of my job absolutely, positively, could *never* be done by a robot, streamlined by a software algorithm, or outsourced to cheap foreign labor?

This is a powerful question to ponder. For real estate agents, the answer has a surprising correlation with the sales cycle (sometimes called a sales funnel). The higher up you go, the more you are hedged against disruptive technologies.

Technology can only automate tasks that *can be automated.* This may sound overly simplistic, but often times real estate agents forget that most of the stuff that can (and eventually will) be automated is the type of work that agents hate doing anyways.

Here's what cannot be automated: cultivating relationships, creating unique marketing campaigns, and building a local brand.

In other words, *trust cannot be automated.*

The more you focus on building trust with potential clients, the safer you are against sudden shocks of innovation (like those that disrupted the travel agent industry).

Like most things in life, it's always better to take the long-term approach. Quality over quantity!

This is why it's so dangerous to follow the transactional approach: by exclusively targeting the low hanging fruit at the "bottom of the funnel," transactional agents are exposing themselves to the collateral damage of innovation.

In the second decade of the 21st century, spending all of your time at the bottom of the real estate funnel is like a horse and buggy company refusing to invest in automobiles in the first decade of the 20th century. Whether you like it or not, changes are coming. Are you ready?

Transactional agents discount the future value of relationships for the present value of a commission check.

What they spend their mornings doing—cold calling potential buyers and sellers—is the exact type of work that will soon become automated. Agents that operate with a short-term transactional mindset, regardless of their hustle and ambition, could be devastated by technology and automation.

The bottom of the funnel is dangerous. It's the most likely place for disruptive technology to automate agents out of a job. However, the earlier in the sales cycle that you focus your time, the more lucrative the investment becomes. Focusing your time at the top of the funnel offers a rare combination: decreased risk with increased returns.

In other words, cultivating the high hanging fruit reduces your risk and increases your rewards.

Usually, these investment criteria have a clear correlation: high-risk investments promise the opportunity of high returns. This is how hedge funds are able to create outlier results for their affluent clients. The opposite is also true: "safe" investments like bonds have "safe" returns.

The *top of the funnel* is the exception to the rule. Dollar for dollar, it creates higher returns with less risk than other investments. It's not nearly as expensive (lower cost per lead). There is also less competition. The only compromise is a trade-off in the time it takes to recover your initial investment. Obviously, if you target prospects that may not be ready to take action for three months, it may be three months before you show a paper profit.

Of course, this is a small price to pay for a competitive advantage that almost guarantees a steady supply of buyers, listings, and referrals.

As a real estate agent, you *are* an investor. Your capital is your time and your marketing budget. When was the last time you evaluated your asset allocation?

The higher up the tree you climb, the more uniquely human the job becomes. Cultivating the high hanging fruit cannot be automated by software. When you generate leads of potential sellers who may be six months away (or more) from actually listing their home for sale, it requires a unique skillset of relationship building and soft-selling.

This process cannot be automated. Building trust from scratch is a uniquely human endeavor. Therefore, focusing your energy at the top of the funnel is simultaneously a growth *and* a risk-management strategy.

When you pick the high hanging fruit, you can have your cake and eat it, too.

Chapter Ten: The Truth About Real Estate Agents

Do you want to discover the truth about real estate agents?

It is an inconvenient truth. It is a truth that most agents would sharply disagree with. They may even throw down this book and stomp on it. It's an uncomfortable truth. But, nonetheless, it is a truth.

It is not an opinion, a perspective, or a subjective analysis. It is an objective reality. Objective in the same sense that 1+1=2.

Here it is: *it is not hard to be a real estate agent.*

There. I said it.

Before you grab the pitchforks and condemn me as a heretic, consider the public's perception: greedy agents get paid a hefty commission to put a sign in the yard, do some paperwork, and get paid a huge commission.

Right or wrong, it is what it is. For the most part, that's what the public thinks!

Oh, and I should mention that the public's perception is the only one that matters. The customer isn't always right, but they're always paying your bills. Don't forget that.

As marketing legend Robert Collier said many years ago, the most effective advertising strategy is to "join the conversation already going on in your prospect's mind."

In other words, it's a waste of time to try and change people's opinions. Instead, invest your energy leveraging the opinions they already hold.

The best advertising campaigns make the prospect think, "I've always thought that! Finally someone is saying it."

When you tap into beliefs that people already hold, it doesn't feel like marketing. You can bypass their bullshit radar. Instead of being skeptical, *they are interested in learning more.*

It's basic psychology (what psychologists call "confirmation bias"). We like to be told we're right, and we instantly trust people who share our own opinions.

One such opinion is that being a real estate agent is not difficult. Whether you like it or not, that is what the general public believes. If you tap into that belief, you will accelerate the trust building process with potential clients.

Which is another way of saying you will *shorten the sales cycle.*

And, let's be honest—there is some validity to that opinion. In most states, you can get licensed in less than a couple months. Other professionals study their craft for years and years before they officially become licensed (doctors, lawyers, engineers, etc). In most cases, real estate agents can be buying and selling homes within 90 days of entering the industry!

It is not hard to be a real estate agent, but it is hard to be a *successful* real estate agent.

The difference between successful real estate agents and their struggling peers has nothing to do with real estate skills. It is a function of their sales and marketing skills.

Specifically, how well they *communicate* their sales and marketing skills.

You may be a listing expert who sells your inventory quickly and for top dollar, but how effective are you at marketing *yourself?*

When a seller decides to list their home, their hiring criteria is simple: they want to work with a marketing expert.

The seller wants to know that the agent will proactively promote the home. The seller wants to know that the agent will create *exposure* for the home.

They are hiring a real estate agent in the same way that a business hires an ad agency: the job of the agency is to enrich the client!

So STOP branding yourself as an expert real estate agent, and START branding yourself as a real estate *marketing expert.* There is a profound difference.

Beyond the branding, you need to really believe it yourself. Stop thinking of yourself as an expert real estate agent, a "top producer," or whatever fancy phrase you've used in the past. Potential clients don't care about your real estate knowledge or experience—they want a marketing expert.

From now on, commit yourself to being a professional marketing expert....*who just happens to specialize in real estate.*

See the difference?

Once you adopt this identity as your new "brand," people WILL notice. You will no longer be just like all the other agents. You will no longer be in marketing no-man's-land: the land of *commodity.*

To successfully pick the high hanging fruit, you must escape commodity status. It is imperative. Nothing else you do will make a more profound impact on your business than escaping the commodity label.

People don't respect commodity products. They don't have brand loyalty to commodity products. They buy whatever is most convenient, or has the cheapest price.

Think of the last time you "shopped" for a commodity product like gasoline...did you actually care about the brand name or the reputation? Of course not. You simply went to the nearest or cheapest gas station. You had minimal expectations of quality or service—you just wanted the lowest price.

Is that the type of prospect you want to attract?

NO!

You want to cultivate enthusiastic leads that want to work with *you, specifically.*

Most of the frustration that agents have with advertising is caused by *what they are advertising.* Their boring ads simply reinforce the stereotype that all real estate agents are the same. They include their picture, phone number, website, and maybe a cheesy slogan. When you look at the typical ads put out by real estate agents, it's not surprising that the public thinks agents are a commodity.

Prove them wrong.

Once you escape commodity status, your income will accelerate. Instead of begging for business, potential clients will beg to work with you. Listing appointments will become a formality. "Random" referrals will increasingly become a larger part of your business.

People want to work with experts. It's true of both seller and buyer clients. It's a trust "shortcut." Instead of going through the lengthy process of getting to know someone, consumers prefer to make a quick decision based on your reputation.

While it may seem like a "fluffy" marketing intangible, expert status is more valuable than any asset on your balance sheet!

The truth about real estate agents is that most of them choose to be a commodity. They choose boring, uninspiring marketing messages. They choose to promote themselves as a real estate agent instead of a professional marketer.

It's a choice.

To pick the high hanging fruit, you must effectively communicate how you're different from other agents.

As Sally Hogshead says, "Different is better than better."

The truth about real estate agents is that it's not hard to be a real estate agent. So don't be one....be a professional marketer *who just happens to specialize in real estate.*

Chapter Eleven: Would You Rather Be Famous Or Rich?

Many real estate agents make the mistake of spending money on *indirect* marketing. Indirect marketing is marketing that hopes to produce a result...indirectly.

Sometimes this is referred to as "branding." There is no call to action, no deadline, and no *offer.*

Most real estate advertisements are what I call a "business card" advertisement. They feature a photo of the agent, the agent's phone number, email, and usually their website. Often there is a cheesy tagline like "I hold the keys to your success," or vague statements such as "Committed To Excellent Service."

The reason I refer to these advertisements as "business card ads" is that they resemble a typical business card. Often they are the same size as a business card. More importantly, they offer very little information that could be considered valuable to the consumer.

Real estate websites are no different.

It's as if the agent gave their business card to a web designer and said, "Here, take this information and turn it into a website."

Most business card ads simply promote a photo of the agent with their relevant contact information—as if seeing the agent's face should compel the prospect to pick up the phone and schedule an appointment!

If you stop and think about this, it's pretty arrogant. It implies that you think seeing your beautiful face is a compelling enough reason to call you.

It's not.

When designing your ads, you have a simple choice to make: would you rather be famous or rich?

Most agents think that the key to success is being famous. It's not. No one will remember your face, your logo, or your contact information. It will be lost in the noise of the thousands of ads that consumers see on a daily basis, *unless your ad offers something of value to the prospect.*

If you want to be rich, use your advertising as an opportunity to create value for potential buyers and sellers. Offer them something they want in exchange for their contact information (a free video series, a PDF download, a book, a list of active homes in a certain price range, etc).

Effective ads always make a *direct offer*. When there is a direct offer of free information, the prospect knows what to do. There is no ambiguity! If they want your free book/video/whatever you're offering, they know exactly how to get it.

The expectation is clear. And when there is no confusion, there will be better conversion.

Inversely, confusion kills conversion.

If you want to increase the effectiveness of your advertising and generate more leads, stop worrying about your "brand awareness." There is only ONE METRIC that determines the failure or success of an ad: the number of leads it generates.

Of course, this illuminates the obvious problem with indirect "branding" ads: if they don't contain a *specific* offer with a *specific* call to action, how will you know if they generated any leads?

The answer is simple: you won't.

If the goal of the ad is to generate local "brand awareness" (become famous), it will be impossible to measure and therefore improve your advertising.

Being famous is subjective. The number of leads an ad generates is objective. How can you quantify the branding value of a $100 ad? You can't! But you *can* measure the effectiveness of a $100 ad if it makes a direct offer to interested prospects.

If 16 people sign up for more information, then the ad produced leads for $6.25 apiece (100/16). These initial numbers provide a "control" for future experiments, which in the marketing world are called *split-tests.*

Understand that measuring your marketing is the foundation of the high hanging fruit philosophy. You cannot build a marketing pipeline randomly. It must be designed.

And the best way to do this is to drive potential prospects to a custom "landing page."

A *landing page* is a simple, one-page website with one goal: get the prospect to sign up with their contact information (usually just name and email).

Let's say you're a real estate agent in Gary, Indiana. If you are offering a free video series on how to buy a home in Gary, you could launch a custom landing like www.BeforeYouBuyInGary.com.

The sole purpose of your ad is to get potential prospects to visit that website! That's it. Nothing else matters. The website should be larger and more prominent than your name, logo, or anything else in the ad.

Remember: the goal of the ad is not to become famous, it's to generate actual *leads.*

The best landing pages are intuitive: the title of the page is self-explanatory. If you visit *BeforeYouBuyInGary.com,* you assume it will contain information about what you need to know before buying a home in Gary.

Pretty simple, right?

The more convincing your ad is, the more people will visit the landing page. This is why it's so important to promise something valuable if they visit your landing page— prospects have better things to do than visit your website just for fun. But if there's something in it for them (like a free video series, book, etc), then they will check it out!

Free, valuable information is the most powerful lead generation strategy in the history of marketing. It works in every industry on Earth.

This technique will make you rich, and it might just make you famous in the process.

Chapter Twelve: A Simple Lead Generation Formula (And 3 Specific Examples Of Ads That Are Working Right Now)

Real estate *used to be* about information. It *used to be* about having access to "the book," where you could view the active listings. Not anymore.

Today, access to information is no longer the product. It's the "bait." People expect information to be free, which is why it's increasingly difficult to get online leads to "register" to view listings, even if you're just asking for name and email.

Why?

In every other industry, this kind of information is freely accessible. *It's not guarded by a registration process.*

If you want to search for books online, Amazon doesn't require you to create an account just to view the inventory. If you want to see the showtimes at a local movie theater, you aren't forced to register with your name and email.

Access to information is not a battle that real estate agents should try to win. There are better, smarter ways to generate leads.

As a 21st century real estate agent, you are not selling information. Those days are long gone! The sales reality of the new millennium empowers the buyer, not the seller. With more choices (and information) than ever, consumers now control the sales process. This is true of all industries, all products, and all services. It's especially true in real estate!

Having access to information is approaching the moral status of food and water. It's an implicit human right. *So good luck trying to use it as a bargaining chip in the sales process.* If you require your prospects to fill out lengthy registration forms before they can search for homes, they'll just ignore you. And they'll find an agent (or website) who gives them the information they want...for free.

You can't beat free.

No matter how hard you try, how many marketing gimmicks you come up with, you can't compete with free.

To survive as a real estate agent in the 21st century, you cannot sell a product your customers can get elsewhere for free. That's not just a difficult sale to make—it's downright impossible.

And you should stop trying.

It's a better use of your time (and money) to sell the ultimate product of the new millennium: **trust**.

The trust that you have your clients' best interests in mind. Trust that you are the most skilled listing agent. Trust that you can sell your clients' homes for a higher price. Trust that you find your buyers the best deals. Trust that you know how to negotiate. Trust that you will get the job done.

In a world where the old deliverables (access to the MLS) are offered for free, trust is the new currency.

In this new economy, your income as a real estate agent will be a direct function of the number of people who trust you.

Before listings were publicly available online, the primary value of working with a real estate agent wasn't market knowledge, negotiating skill, or advice. It was simply a monopoly on information.

Licensed agents had access to the listings. Buyers and sellers did not. It was that simple.

But it wasn't, and isn't, just about access to listings. Licensed real estate agents used to have a practical monopoly on other information, too! Things like mortgage calculators, homebuying tips, selling advice, and pricing strategies were all proprietary. Before the Internet, potential clients couldn't just search for blog articles about home staging tips or house hunting advice...they had to seek out a licensed real estate agent.

Everything started and ended with contacting an agent.

Those days are long gone. It's been over twenty years since real estate agents enjoyed a monopoly on information (1994 was the last year that listings were *not* available online).

Strangely enough, most agents pretend as if this never happened. They still operate their businesses as if they are in control of the sales process, not the client. They falsely believe that buyers and sellers need them more than they need buyers and sellers.

This used to be true, but it is no longer the case.

The budgets of most agents reflect this mistake. They are not investing in building a list of prospects, nor are they investing in cultivating their existing database. In fact, most agents invest hardly anything into marketing. They are completely delusional when it comes to 21st century client acquisition.

This is like a fisherman placing a bucket on the dock, and expecting fish to jump out of the water and straight into the bucket.

You're probably not going to catch a lot of fish this way!

The inescapable truth is that almost every real estate agent chronically underinvests in marketing.

If you look at top producers, one thing almost all of them have in common is a commitment to aggressive investment in lead generation. They don't wait for business to come to them; they go out and get it. And they're willing to pay the necessary acquisition costs—it's a business, not a hobby.

There are two main reasons that agents underinvest in marketing. The first—and most common—is a discouraging return on investment from previous marketing expenditures. The second reason is that most agents can create a 6-figure income *without relying on advertising.* With hard work and a few referrals, it is possible to earn over $100,000/year as a real estate agent.

In fact, most agents can crack the "six figure" mark without any investment in paid advertising!

Unfortunately, this is where most agents plateau.

It's a classic case of *what got you here won't get you there.* To scale your business beyond this level, you cannot simply work harder. If you're already working 60 hours a week, doubling your income is not as simple as doubling your hours. No one can work 120 hours a week! Hustle can create momentum, but marketing systems can create leverage.

If you're accustomed to (not) investing in marketing, it feels like you're *losing control* of your business when you start spending thousands of dollars on lead generation. Ironically, this couldn't be further from the truth: the ability to create your own leads—and therefore create your own income—is the ultimate form of control.

If you've never invested in paid advertising, it might feel painful at first. Keep in mind that everyone invests in business growth one way or another. Even if you've never spent a dollar on paid advertising, you have still invested your *time*. Unless you value your time at zero, this is a significant investment!

Because most agents forget that their time is worth X/hour, they think that their business has grown "organically." And so the idea of spending any money on advertising seems unnecessary.

The truth is that the investment required to close 25-30 transactions per year is mostly time. Up until that milestone, the main ingredient is hustle.

After that point, hustle is necessary, but it's not *sufficient.* To take your real estate business to the next level, you will need to leverage paid advertising.

Both time and money are investments, but time cannot scale. Money can.

Unfortunately, when they start spending money on ads, most agents experience minimal success. This merely reinforces their belief that advertising "just doesn't work."

Most agents waste money on print ads, billboards, online ads, and mailers that don't produce leads. Their ads have no *call to action*. There is no reason to respond. As a result, little to no leads are generated.

The implicit goal of these ads is to build a brand by "getting your name out there." For local real estate agents, this simply does not work! Massive, billion dollar companies like McDonalds or Nike can afford an indirect branding strategy, but local real estate agents must hold every dollar accountable. Every dollar must produce results. Every ad should produce a certain amount of leads, and this metric should be ruthlessly measured and optimized.

For example, before purchasing a $500 print advertisement in the local newspaper, you should have a clear and unambiguous method of tracking the results. How many leads did it generate? The number of impressions, views, or readership are fluff metrics that provide zero value for the agent. The only thing that matters is the number of actual leads.

In other words, how many prospects saw your ad, and as a direct result of the ad, took a specific action like calling your office or signing up with their name & email for more information?

The goal of any marketing expenditure—whether it's in the newspaper, on Facebook, or direct mail—is the generation of actual leads that can be followed up with. Period. There are no bonus points awarded for "exposure," "branding," or fluff metrics that don't directly produce leads.

Exposure does not pay the bills. Branding does not pay the bills. As a real estate agent, you only get paid for successful closings, and closings are the result of actual leads. Branding that does not result in immediate leads is worthless; real estate is not a popularity contest! The goal of marketing is not to be the most recognizable face. The goal is to attract viable leads with compelling advertising that convinces buyer and sellers to actually contact you.

The best way to do this is to offer something of actual value. This is simultaneously the most simple and most powerful marketing strategy in the world: offer something valuable in exchange for people's contact information.

That's it. It really is that simple. There's no need to complicate things....just give away something buyers and sellers want, and ask them to "pay" for it by trading you their contact information.

Instead of *buying* the valuable information you're offering, you're proposing a trade. No money changes hands. Just ask the prospects to sign up with their name & email address (maybe phone number), and you'll give them access to something they want.

The effectiveness of your advertising is merely a function of how valuable the thing is that you're giving away. If it has a high perceived value, your marketing will be incredibly effective. If it doesn't, it won't.

Simple, right?

I've seen local real estate marketing campaigns produce leads for just a dollar apiece. That's right....spend $100 dollars, get 100 new prospects!

The key to generating maximum leads for minimum money has nothing to do with where or how you run an advertisement. It could be on Facebook, it could be in the newspaper, it could be on the radio, or maybe even a targeted direct mail campaign.

What's most important is the *offer*: what are you offering in exchange for people's contact information? If it's something that buyers and sellers really want to know, they will gladly sign up. It's not like you're asking them to pay $100 to access your deliverable. It's free—all you're asking for is their email address!

The abysmal results of most real estate advertising is a direct reflection of the poorly thought out offers.

So, what's your offer? What *should be* your offer?

Let's start with what not to offer: ambiguity. Ambiguity is vague and uninspiring. Yet this is exactly what most agents "offer" in their advertisements.

- *Call me to get started.*
- *Visit my website for more information.*
- *Contact us today!*

Almost all real estate ads are variations of these three "calls to action." It should not be surprising that almost all real estate advertising is completely, utterly ineffective! None of these "calls to action" promise anything specific.

A far better approach is to offer something tangible and specific, and give clear instructions on how to get it:

To Discover The Current Market Value Of Your Home, Check Out www.LexingtonHomePrices.com

To attract buyers, the same thinking applies: you must offer something tangible and specific, and give clear instructions on how to get it:

Find Out If You Qualify For The Zero-Down Mortgage Program: Take Our 5-Minute HomeBuyer Quiz at www.LexingtonHomeBuyerQuiz.com

The possibilities are endless. Ask yourself: what can I offer in my advertisements that buyers and sellers *actually want?* Sellers want to know the current market value of their home. They want specific advice on how to maximize the sales price of their home. They want help in choosing an agent who is a marketing expert that will aggressively promote their listing (the number one complaint of sellers is that their agent didn't do enough to promote the property).

Similarly, there are a handful of things that buyers want: they want advice on how to pick a home, how to increase the likelihood that they qualify for the right mortgage, the characteristics of different neighborhoods. Lead generation is as simple as delivering what they want, and asking for their contact information as "payment."

You could write a quick 5-page PDF report on the different neighborhoods in your town. You could film a quick video on the latest mortgage program that makes it easier to buy a home. You could create a list of all the recent sold listings in a certain zip code, and offer it in the context of a "Homeowner's Property Value Report." All of the above would make great lead generation offers, because they contain valuable information that buyers and sellers want to know *before they buy or sell.*

This is the key to the high hanging fruit philosophy: attract buyers and sellers before they are actually ready to buy or sell. If a seller is planning on listing their home next week, they probably aren't interested in a free report on home staging tips....*because they're probably already working with an agent.*

However, if your free offer of information appeals to them earlier in the sales cycle, they will gladly sign up. Pick the high hanging fruit!

Create your lead generation offers based on what buyers and sellers want. It really is that simple!

Here are three proven lead generation ideas that are currently being used by Platform™ clients all around the country:

- **1.) Write a book about your local real estate market.** For example, *The Ultimate Guide To Lexington Real Estate.* Offer your "free book" in advertisements. To receive the book, prospects simply need to fill out a contact form so you know where to send the book (this is a great way to gather detailed contact information without it seeming like you're trying to gather contact information). The fastest way to "write" a book is to record yourself talking (like a podcast), and then have the audio transcribed into text. I recommend using castingwords.com. They charge $1/minute of audio, so a 90-minute audio recording would cost just $90 to be transcribed into words. 90 minutes of audio will create around 75 pages of content in a book. While it sounds like a lot of time, it's actually quite easy to talk about your local real estate market for 90 minutes. Just spend an hour drafting a rough outline of what you want to cover (topics like how to stage your home to sell, the importance of curb appeal, the importance of getting pre-approved, how to improve your credit score, why it's important to not max out your budget and become "house poor," etc. Sprinkle in advice and insights that are locally specific, so readers know you are a local real estate agent. As an added bonus, claiming that you *literally* "wrote the book" on local real estate is an incredibly powerful marketing message. Buyers and sellers want to work with a professional, expert agent: what better way to position yourself as an authority than by writing a book? After all, the root word of "authority" is....*author.*

2.) Film video tours of your listings (not picture slideshows), and have interested prospects sign up before being allowed to view the video tours. This is a tactic we use with all of our Platform™ clients (who pay us $18,000/year to fully manage their lead generation and marketing). If that doesn't convince you it's worth trying, I don't know what will! Launch a specific website for every listing you film. If the property address is 1347 Oak Ridge Lane, set up a website called www.1347OakRidgeLane.com. At that website, prospects are asked to enter their name and email to get access to the video. Anyone willing to enter their contact information to watch the video has implicitly raised their hand and said, "Yes! I'm interested in buying this home!" *If they weren't an interested buyer, they wouldn't have signed up for the video.* This is a perfect "qualifier" to ensure that you are generating quality leads.

3.) Promote an online "quiz" to help potential sellers figure out if they should sell their home. Again, this is a tool we use with all of our Platform™ clients. If they are willing to pay $18,000/year to have this implemented for them, it's worth trying! The most important part of this ad is the psychology behind it: no one wants to fill out a "form" or an "application," but they are usually willing to answer those same questions *in the context of a quiz.* Questions might include "How long have you lived in your home, " or "Have you recently upgraded the bathroom and/or kitchen?" Potential sellers are happy to take the quiz because they want to find out if they're in a good position to sell their home. At the conclusion of the quiz—after they've spent 5 minutes or more of their time answering the questions—ask for a name and email to complete the quiz. *To see their results, they must enter this contact information.* The perceived "sunk cost" of the time they invested convinces most prospects to enter their contact information. These are extremely valuable seller leads!

Hopefully these three ad templates inspire you to create compelling offers in your local advertising. I have personally spent $100,000+ on testing and tweaking these ads. I know they work. The reason is simple: *they offer something that people actually want.*

I cannot emphasize this enough: it is easy to generate leads when you give something away that buyers and sellers actually want.

If your ads "aren't working," it's because your offer is unappealing. That's it. Nothing more, nothing less.

Chapter Thirteen: How To Apply The Silicon Valley "Growth Hacking" Strategy To Your Local Real Estate Business

Would you like to discover a marketing "secret" that has launched multiple billion-dollar companies?

In 2014, Ryan Holiday published a short book about a new trend in the world of tech startups: *growth hacking*. Borrowing from the ideas of software marketers like Andrew Chen and Sean Ellis, Ryan's book was an early manifesto for the growth hacker movement.

(The book, *Growth Hacker Marketing*, is available on Amazon for less than $10)

The idea was simple: what if marketers started acting less like artists and more like scientists?

How would that change their promotional strategy?

Traditionally, a product "launch" was the business equivalent of a Hollywood blockbuster campaign. Billboards would be purchased, newspaper ads placed, and TV commercials produced. With this traditional mindset, you'd go big or go home.

Millions of dollars were spent on promoting something in a big way, all at once. The risks were enormous.

Here's the strange part: marketers knew that a high percentage of these campaigns would fail, *and they didn't care.* They were hoping that the few campaigns that did work were so successful that they covered the costs of the losers.

In other words, it was a venture capital approach to marketing. You had no idea what was going to work, so you diversified your risk across as many investments as possible. In the end, you hoped that the profits from the winners exceeded the losses from the losers.

It was an expensive way to play the game.

This is how Hollywood movie studios operate. Since they can't predict the future, they don't know which movies will bomb, which movies will break even, or which movies will make hundreds of millions of dollars (sometimes even *billions*).

So they dump lots of money into each movie release, cross their fingers, and hope for the best.

The long-term winners are the producers who have managed to produce more blockbuster successes than blockbuster failures.

It's only slightly less risky than high stakes gambling.

"Growth hacking" eliminates this problem, once and for all.

The *growth hacking* movement is beginning to change how companies think about their marketing strategy. As far as I know, no one has applied this revolutionary approach to the world of real estate.

If you're reading this book, you have a significant head start on the competition. It will take them at least a couple years to realize the shift that is happening in the marketing world.

In my estimation, most marketing trends take 5-10 years to catch on in the real estate industry. Sometimes even longer!

For example, even though it's 2015 (you may be reading this book in 2016, 2017, and beyond), many real estate agents *still do not have a functional website.*

(Having a personal page within your broker's website does not count as having a website anymore than borrowing your friend's car means you own a vehicle!)

Even though it's 2015, many real estate agents still do not use social media proactively to generate and convert leads.

Even though it's 2015, many real estate agents still do not actively use a CRM to manage their database.

Even though it's 2015, many real estate agents still do not use video to promote their listings. This last one is absolutely *crazy* considering that the world's second largest search engine is.....YouTube.

(I'll share some specific strategies on that later!)

The list goes on and on. The real estate profession is almost allergic to innovation.

So, it's probably safe to say that a contrarian strategy that's still viewed as "fringe" in the world of professional marketing will take *at least* a couple more years to catch the attention of local real estate agents.

Obviously, this is an incredible opportunity!

Until now, growth hacking has been a mostly underground movement in the marketing world. Corporate marketers at Fortune 500 companies dismissed it as the latest "fad." Notable *billion dollar* case studies attributable to growth hacking were ignored, because it seemed to contradict everything they thought they knew about marketing.

Of course, this is how innovation works. It's disruptive to the status quo. It's uncomfortable. It makes you question even your most basic assumptions about how (and why) things work.

It's probably a decent litmus test for new initiatives: if a new business idea makes you extremely uncomfortable, you should act on it!

The maximum level of discomfort you initially tolerate will be the minimum level of discomfort your competitors are forced to endure when you implement the idea.

Reacting to a change in the competitive landscape is always harder than creating the change.

For real estate agents brave enough to borrow some trade secrets from Silicon Valley, the "underground" world of growth hacking presents one such opportunity.

What if you started treating your real estate career as less of a professional *hobby* and more of a *business*?

What if you started measuring everything?

And I mean everything.

The number of leads you get per month, the number of emails you send, the number of opened emails, the conversion rate on your landing pages, the CTR of your ads, the percentage of prospects who answer when you call/text, etc. Some metrics are more important than others, but the central truth of growth hacking is that metrics are important to begin with.

A growth hacker borrows the best practices of computer programmers, data scientists, and professional marketers. A growth hacker completely (and unequivocally) embraces *data*, not luck. Intuition can lead to innovation, but growth hacking can refine those ideas into true breakthroughs.

Here are some examples of growth hacking for real estate agents:

- A real estate agent in Colorado was able to generate viable seller leads (with name, email, and phone number) for less than ten dollars apiece after split-testing three different headlines, and six different images on a Facebook ad.
- A real estate agent in Wisconsin generated buyer leads for less than a dollar apiece by testing different demographics in his ad targeting. The best audience turned out to be newly engaged couples and newlyweds.
- A real estate agent in Maryland used a "quiz" to attract interested sellers. After multiple failed attempts, he finally discovered a new online ad format that cut the cost per lead in half. The breakthrough came when he upped the age limit (targeting ages 35+), and optimized his ad for social media engagement, NOT website clicks. The increased engagement

naturally led to more website clicks, which in turn generated a steady flow of listings.

- A real estate agent in Kentucky used a new landing page that tripled the conversion rate of her listing ad (the breakthrough came by split-testing a white background versus a photo background). In other tests, a video background created even better results!

I can verify the validity of these case studies, because *I was the scientist conducting the experiments.* These are all case studies of my clients using the Platform™ system.

Because we have embraced the "growth hacker" mindset, our clients have a huge advantage over their local competition. We measure *everything*, so our clients benefit from a constant process of iteration.

You can't manage what you can't measure!

Of course, growth hacking is more than just "split testing." The idea of split testing has been around since Claude Hopkins published the book *Scientific Advertising* way back in 1923.

Growth hacking, at its core, takes a renewed interest in the product itself. Growth hackers reject the "dualistic" philosophy inherent in most marketing plans.

Dualism is the tendency of most marketers to think of product development as completely separate from product promotion.

This mindset essentially says, "Hey guys, the engineers created a cool product. Now it's your turn to design a killer ad campaign to sell it!"

Growth hacking is a refusal to separate the promotion from the product. In fact, quite the opposite: the best way to optimize the marketing is to *optimize the product itself.*

It's always better to have a good product with a tiny advertising budget than a poor product with a big advertising budget. When the deliverable doesn't meet the customer's expectations, a hefty marketing budget simply spreads the bad news faster.

This truth is amplified in a relationship business like real estate.

This is where many real estate agents get mixed up— they think the product is the listings they are selling. This couldn't be further from the truth.

When it comes to selecting a real estate agent (the only "buying" decision that actually matters to the agent), buyers and sellers don't care about what's currently available on the market. They don't perform exhaustive research on price per square foot of X neighborhood versus Y neighborhood, sales volume trends, or the general direction of the *days on market* statistics.

They expect their real estate agent to handle all of these details. They don't want to get lost in the economic details of the housing market. Whether they're buying or selling, the only decision they want to make is what real estate agent to trust *to make all of their other decisions for them.*

Obviously, the client will ultimately select the home they want to purchase. The agent cannot choose for them. But they will lean on the recommendations and insight of their agent when making that decision. Most buyers and sellers are not ignorant of this process—*they know what they don't know.*

They are looking for someone to trust. This is an inherently intuitive decision. No amount of fancy PowerPoint slideshows or sales statistics can replace the primal feeling of *trust.*

When they trot in a few agents to interview for the privilege of listing their home, it's not as if sellers are using a complex mathematical formula to select the winner.

Not even close.

In reality, buyers and sellers choose which agent to work with based on feelings. Similar to economic figures like GDP, trust is an aggregate metric that is the sum of many different variables.

When choosing an agent, buyers and sellers will consider things like:

- Does the agent have a beautiful website?
- Is the website updated with helpful information?
- Does the agent appear to be successful?
- Does the agent have a sizable list of testimonials?
- Can I trust the agent to actually promote my listing?
- Does he/she have an aggressive marketing plan?
- Can I trust them to act in my best interest?

Trust is what they're buying, so it better be what you're selling!

Let's face it: being a real estate agent is not hard. Of course, I'm not saying it's easy to make money as a real estate agent. *That's* the hard part!

The struggle is in the lead generation and conversion. What separates top producers from everyone else is their commitment to excellence in *sales and marketing*! It really doesn't have anything to do with how good they are at being a real estate agent.

Top producers aren't magically better at showing homes to their buyers, nor do their listings somehow sell faster (unless they aggressively invest in paid ads). Being a top producer really has nothing to do with how "good" you are at real estate. It has everything to do with *how good you are at marketing yourself* as a real estate agent.

See the difference?

The actual "day to day" responsibilities of the job are not particularly difficult: showing homes to buyers, researching comps, uploading data to the MLS, etc.

There's a reason it usually takes less than a month in most states to get licensed as a real estate agent. It's not rocket science. You don't need a master's degree or a bachelor's degree to be a successful real estate agent. In fact, sometimes higher education can be a hindrance if it interferes with the necessary "street smarts" learned on the job.

The doing of the job is not what grows your business, it's the marketing of how you do your job.

Especially in our modern age of social media, people *will* talk about your product. So give them something to talk about!

The principles of growth hacking tell us that marketing is futile unless you have *something worth marketing.* The advertisement itself is much less important than the perceived value of what is being advertised.

That's YOU.

For example, when you go on listing appointments, do you have an in-depth proprietary marketing plan? Ideally, this plan is branded as if it were a product. For example, the *Bob Smith 27 Point Marketing Plan*, which details the twenty-seven specific promotional strategies you use to promote your listings.

Don't just hand the prospect a 3-ring binder with a bunch of boring fluff about your broker—give them a "product" to purchase.

Of course, the product being purchased here is trust. If you have a proprietary 27-Point Marketing Plan (ideally with its own website, ie www.BobSmithMarketingPlan.com), the sellers know they can trust you. You are uniquely positioned as an expert marketer. No amount of salesmanship on the part of other agents can overcome the fact that you have a detailed, expertly designed *plan* to sell homes. This is a level of professionalism and excellence that is rare in the real estate industry.

And it's magnetic. My clients tell me all the time that when they show sellers their proprietary marketing plan, they can sense a shift in the sales energy of the conversation.

All of a sudden the seller is actually paying attention! They were bored out of their mind when shown the canned content from their broker's template presentation, but the proprietary marketing plan was something tangible. It was specific. It *differentiated* them from other agents, and therefore gave the seller a logical reason to choose them.

It's the perfect answer to the question the seller is secretly struggling to answer: *why should I choose you over the other agents I'm interviewing to list my home?*

Don't leave the decision up to the emotional whims of the seller: give them a logical reason to choose you! A proprietary, branded marketing plan proves that you are an expert real estate marketer. That's a powerful reason, both emotionally *and* logically.

Of course, such a marketing plan is just a tangible manifestation of the real product being bought and sold in a listing appointment: trust.

From the perspective of the real estate agent, this means that you must treat every client like gold. Even if it's an annoying client who tours twelve homes before they make a lowball offer on a rambler listed at $135,000....you must treat them as if they're a million dollar cash buyer.

Why?

Because you never know who they are connected to. That annoying buyer whose potential commission isn't worth your time might know someone with a massive social media audience. Maybe a local journalist or blogger. If you don't provide excellent customer service, not only will you miss out on potential referrals, you may just be the recipient of a damning blog post that's read by thousands of potential clients.

Potential clients that will no longer work with you after reading the review!

While it sounds harsh, this is the new reality. Social media is not going away. No longer is it enough to have mediocre products and services that are subsidized by expensive marketing campaigns.

This is growth hacking 101: focus on *optimizing the product,* and the marketing will take care of itself.

While most people would admit that a poor product cannot be saved by good marketing, they think that mediocre, average products can be salvaged.

I disagree.

"Average" is the worst positioning of all. It's an issue of math—all the competition is in the middle! When you have a mediocre product, you are competing with 90% of the market that also produces mediocrity.

It would be much better to serve the bottom five percent or the top five percent.

There's less competition at the top. Pick the high hanging fruit!

Of course, real estate agents aren't selling "products." They don't have the benefit of choosing which widgets to promote. They must sell their listings, regardless of their condition. Some sellers refuse to update old carpets, ugly paint, or embarrassingly outdated bathrooms. And, for the most part, there is nothing a real estate agent can do about this.

The quality of the "product" is out of the agent's control. Most agents will take any listing, no matter how outdated or overpriced, if the alternative is no listing at all. The quality of their product is a metric they can't afford to manage.

What about the quality of the marketing itself?

Here is a real estate marketing breakthrough: you are the product.

The quality of your marketing, not what it is actually promoting, is the product for sale.

For the most part, you can't control what homes you sell. But you can control *how you sell them.*

Growth hackers refer to this as product-market fit. In a nutshell, it's simply making sure that you are offering something that the market actually wants.

Most real estate agents are not.

When they go on listing presentations, they brag about their broker's storied history, how many transactions they've closed in the last ten years, the millions of dollars in transaction volume, blah, blah, blah.

This is jargon, and the seller does not care!

From the perspective of your "customer" (the seller), the only thing that matters is what you are going to do to sell *their* home.

They are not buying your broker, your website, or fancy PowerPoint listing presentation. They are buying your marketing plan. If they believe you have a better marketing plan than other agents, you will get the listing.

It's really that simple.

Your product is your marketing plan, and the best way to increase sales is to increase your product quality: you must improve your marketing plan.

Why should someone list their home for sale with *you*, and not the other agents that want the listing?

Do you have a compelling answer to this question?

Commit to becoming the best real estate marketer in your entire city. When you do, you'll find that you're organically attracting more warm referrals (as well as an increased conversion on your "cold" lead generation).

As a local real estate agent, you can spend all the money in the world on promotion, but the most important ingredient is always *what you're promoting in the first place.*

No amount of split tests can optimize mediocrity. You must start with optimizing the actual product. Paid advertising is just icing on the cake.

The growth hacking philosophy dictates that a dollar spent on product development is worth ten dollars spent on advertising. Or maybe even a hundred!

One of my favorite growth hacking case studies is the story of Hotmail. Before modern tech companies like Facebook, LinkedIn, and Uber, growth hacking techniques made Hotmail a household name.

For *free.*

The Hotmail story is almost legendary amongst growth hackers, because one simple tweak created a billion dollar market. And in hindsight, it was so obvious!

But in 1996, it wasn't. The growth hacking philosophy had not yet been developed. Marketers still adhered to the traditional strategy of "spend a bunch of money on ads and hope something works."

But Hotmail was a startup. They didn't have millions of dollars to waste on billboards or Super Bowl ads. According to Ryan Holiday's account in *Growth Hacker Marketing*, they launched with just $300,000 in startup capital. So instead of spending millions and millions of dollars on traditional paid advertising campaigns, the Hotmail team put a simple message in the signature of every email:

PS

Get your free email at Hotmail.

Including this line at the bottom of every message transformed each email into an advertisement. And it was the best kind of advertisement: an implied testimonial.

The idea worked. Hotmail exploded in growth, adding over one million users in the first six months. The company was eventually sold to Microsoft for a whopping $400 million dollars.

This is the essence of growth hacking: *building viral features into the product itself.*

To be clear, growth hacking is not a random attempt to create products and "hope" they somehow go viral (whatever that means). It is a new way of *thinking* about marketing. Growth hacking is a collection of proven principles that can be applied in any industry.

As you probably guessed, you can use these same techniques in your real estate marketing.

Ask yourself: what are you currently creating that is so cool, people would share it *for* you?

Money solves most business problems, but you cannot buy your way out of an uninteresting product. If anything, money makes the problem worse. The more you spend advertising your mediocrity, the more people will find out!

Instead of throwing more money at the problem, address the root issue (not the symptom). That is, think about the product itself.

Here's how I would get started: build virality into your marketing plan.

Create content worth talking about: film professional videos of all listings, take professional photography of all listings, and treat each listing like a million dollar property.

People will talk about you *if you give them something to talk about.*

In his controversial book *Purple Cow*, marketing expert Seth Godin defines remarkable marketing literally: marketing that is worth remarking about.

If it's "remarkable," then people will talk about it—that's the definition of the word remarkable!

Worth talking about.

So, ask yourself, are you creating marketing content that is worth talking about? Or are you simply crossing your fingers and hoping something goes viral?

Our Platform™ clients spend hundreds of dollars promoting their listings. Sometimes even thousands of dollars. Why? Because it's not just promoting the property, it's simultaneously promoting *them*. Buyers love seeing the listing ads, and potential sellers do too!

(Not to mention your clients love it when you create massive exposure for their home)

When you invest money in promoting your listing inventory, you are "marketing your marketing."

Growth hacking 101.

Chapter Fourteen: How A Failing Lead Generation Campaign Became Our Best Performing Ad, Overnight

High-income earners, regardless of their industry, usually share one thing in common: a very high transaction value.

It's a pretty simple idea: the top sales producers earning the most money are usually selling expensive products and services.

The best salesman in the world will still struggle to make a middle class income if he is stuck selling consumer electronics at Best Buy. Even though he will make multiple sales per day, there simply isn't a large enough commission per sale to create meaningful income.

And this is an interesting point: highly paid salespeople usually make less frequent, higher dollar sales.

In real estate, sales frequency is a poor measure of success. It's terribly misleading. If all you pay attention to is the number of closings, you are bound to make stupid decisions when it comes to marketing.

Sure, the number of closed transactions is a convenient number to track, but it doesn't tell the whole story. Statistics are like a bikini: what they reveal is suggestive, but what they conceal is vital.

It would be very difficult, if not downright impossible, to make a 6-figure income by selling lots of $100 products. Even if you sold ten per day at a 10% commission, you would only be creating $100/day of income. For most people, this equates to relative poverty.

It really doesn't matter if you go days—or even weeks—without a closing. What matters is how much your closings are worth. Rather than judging the effectiveness of your marketing campaign on a daily basis—or even a weekly basis—evaluate your strategy using a monthly perspective.

Who cares how many leads you generated *today*. Who cares how many leads you generated this *week*. When the business model revolves around $5,000-$10,000 commission checks (or even higher), it is usually meaningless to micromanage results when the sample size is that small.

The greater the potential income, the larger time horizon you should use when evaluating the ROI.

I've worked with many clients who started the Platform™ lead generation program, and became frustrated after a week of no "converted" leads. The campaigns had a favorable cost per click, a solid email open rate, and the client was receiving multiple leads per day! But they had yet to "convert" one of these leads into a buyer or seller client that either listed their home or bought a home.

From their perspective, the return on investment was a big fat ZERO.

And I get it. When you're investing significant resources into a marketing program, you expect tangible results. And you want those results sooner than later!

Adding more likes to your Facebook page doesn't cut it. If you're investing money into generating leads, it's not *the leads* you're paying for. What you want is *closings.*

I get it. Really, I do.

But sometimes focusing on micro results completely distorts how you perceive macro results. In real estate, daily income is meaningless. What's more important is monthly income.

It really doesn't matter if you didn't "convert" any leads this week. Or even next week. What matters is how the marketing math works out on a monthly, or better yet, a *quarterly* basis.

When you think in terms of quarterly ROI instead of weekly ROI, you will begin to understand why so many agents chronically underinvest in marketing.

They don't see immediate results from their ad dollars, and they quit.

This is tantamount to a farmer planting seeds in April, and declaring the business a failure in July because he didn't harvest anything. A farmer has to take a "big picture" perspective on his investment. He can't evaluate it on a daily, weekly, or even monthly basis! Doing so would distort the true return on investment, and cause him to make stupid decisions (like selling his entire field in July for a bargain price).

The same is true in real estate.

Real estate has a natural sales cycle. The vast majority of quality leads will take a couple months of cultivation before they are ready to buy or sell. Unfortunately, search aggregators like Zillow have psychologically brainwashed most agents into thinking if a lead doesn't want to immediately start scheduling showings, it's somehow a bad lead.

This is nonsense. And it presents a massive opportunity for agents who can see the big picture.

Especially when one "conversion" pays for all the ads you're running this month, next month, and the month after that. Some deals are large enough to pay for your entire annual marketing budget!

With a business model where one single sale pays for multiple months of marketing, you don't even need a sale per month to break even. Really, all you need is one sale every other month to break even.

Now, of course, no one is interested in aiming for the bare minimum. Like Jennifer Aniston's waitress character in the movie *Office Space*, breaking even is not an option. We don't want our marketing dollars to simply pay for themselves, we want them to multiply by a factor of ten (or more).

This may seem like a basic idea, but it should change the way you think about your marketing strategy as a real estate agent.

Are you measuring success based on the actual numbers, or warm fuzzy feelings? Are you evaluating the effectiveness of your lead generation strategy with a big picture perspective, or are you micromanaging it with unrealistic daily expectations?

Let's say you are advertising a $400,000 home. For most agents, this will create a commission check around the $10,000 mark. This is an ideal sweet spot price range in most markets—high enough to be worth your time, but low enough to have a fair amount of potential transaction volume.

If you listed a $400,000 home, would you evaluate the effectiveness of your advertising on a daily basis? Would it make any sense, whatsoever, to run a week-long newspaper ad and evaluate it every single day?

Of course not.

You would evaluate the totality of the ad, for the full 7 days it ran, and *then* decide whether or not it was effective.

You wouldn't say, "Monday was a failure, Tuesday was a failure, Wednesday was a failure, Thursday was a failure, Friday was a failure, Saturday was a failure, but Sunday attracted a buyer!"

This is asinine. The evaluation would simply be that *the ad worked.* Period.

You invested in a week's worth of advertising—what particular day attracted a qualified buyer lead is meaningless. You aren't measuring individual days, you are measuring the effectiveness of the overall ad campaign!

Of course, this sounds obvious. But many agents have nothing better to do than micromanage their ad campaigns, because it makes them feel like they are in control of their business.

I have a client named Susan (not her real name) who insists on daily "accountability" of her marketing strategy. Not only is this annoying...it is incredibly *discouraging.*

Susan emails us on an almost daily basis, telling us how many leads she generated that day from our marketing campaigns. Usually, this number is around 5-10. Keep in mind that my team manages her ads for her, so we already know these numbers before she does!

This daily "update' is incredibly discouraging for her. Sure, she is receiving lots of inbound leads (more than a hundred per month), *but most of the time she will not convert a lead into a client the same day it is generated.*

It usually takes a couple weeks (or months) to properly cultivate leads.

For most agents in most markets, all you need is a handful of transactions per month to make a healthy income—this means that a majority of the days you will not "convert" a lead.

Would you label this a success or a failure?

How you answer this question will shape your real estate business.

It can be frustrating going multiple days in a row without converting a new buyer or seller lead, *but not when you consider how much money you're earning on the days that you do convert a lead.*

Taking such a short-term perspective is a guaranteed recipe for stress....which inevitably leads to discouragement. And while discouragement is merely an emotion, emotions are powerful.

Especially for a salesperson.

In a traditional sales profession like real estate, you must become comfortable with rejection. We've all read sales books, attended seminars, and heard speakers lecture about the importance of not taking "no" personally.

In fact, the overwhelming majority of the sales training world can be summarized in this one sentence: don't be afraid of rejection.

How then, in a career selling real estate—where your income is 100% determined by commission—can you possibly expect to thrive if you're constantly discouraged?

You must take a bigger perspective, or you'll miss the forest for the trees. You might even miss the trees for the acorns.

Would you say an agent is a failure if they are closing two transactions per month, at an average pop of $10,000?

It sure *seems like* a failure: two transactions in 30 days. That means 93% of days there are no closings!

Obviously, 93% of the time they aren't converting a lead, but they are making $20,000 per month. $60,000 per quarter.

Not bad for a 93% "failure rate."

Usually I tell my real estate clients to look at their business from a quarterly perspective. Don't get caught up in how much money you spent on ads today, yesterday, last week, or even last month. These intervals are too small a sample size to be statistically significant.

The solution? Look at your real estate business in 90-day increments.

Here's the only question that really matters for real estate agents: how much money did you invest in marketing in the last 90 days, and how much commission did that create?

If you are seeing a positive ROI with your quarterly marketing evaluation, keep doing what you're doing.

(Ideally, leverage your success by further optimizing the ads using split tests)

What you may find is that the first month was a "loss," the second month broke even, but the 3rd month was a smashing success.

Is this a coincidence? Hardly.

Any solid lead generation program will target top funnel leads (the high hanging fruit), who may not be ready to buy or sell for another 30-90 days. It's simply too difficult, and too expensive, to compete with search aggregators at the bottom of the sales cycle (like Zillow).

It's nice receiving buyer leads that are ready to start house hunting *today*, or seller leads that are ready to list their home *today*, but this is unrealistic, unreliable, and above all, unaffordable!

It's a far better strategy to focus on attracting and cultivating leads that aren't ready to buy now, *but will be in the near future.*

Of course, real estate (like any other business) has a natural sales cycle. It's unrealistic to expect a fresh lead to purchase or sell a home within a week of contacting you. Even if they start house hunting immediately, it will be a couple weeks before a closing can be scheduled.

This means that you should not judge an advertising campaign based on its first month. It's simply too small of a sample size.

Don't get me wrong—converting leads within the first month is a terrific goal. It's just usually not a realistic one. We have a word for clients who manage to convert leads in less than 30 days...*lucky.*

And we are up front about this with our new clients: think of quick conversions as icing on the cake.

The real money is made in sticking to a consistent marketing program over the long term, and continuously running split tests to optimize the best performing ads.

The goal is always to bring down the CPL (cost per lead), while simultaneously increasing the number of overall leads. Even small improvements, such as improving the CPL from $8 to $6, can make a profound difference over time. If you were spending $1000/month on ads, this would translate to 25% more leads every single month!

(Unfortunately, some marketing companies cherry pick testimonials based on exceptional clients who immediately converted leads. In a literal sense, these *exceptional* case studies are the exception to the rule.)

So commit this to memory: most marketing programs *worth investing in* will NOT be profitable the first month.

The second month may break even, because usually a lead that was generated during the first 30 days will convert at some point in the second month. Then, all of a sudden, the third month will produce multiple conversions.

Is it a coincidence that this pattern repeats itself with almost every client I've ever worked with? I don't think so.

It's not luck; it's math.

Because of the natural sales cycle, leads generated during the first month will typically convert during months two and three. Leads generated during the second month will usually convert in months three and four.

If you detect a pattern here, you're onto something! Say it with me: leads generated during the third month will convert in months.....four and five. *And so on.* It's a predictable mathematical function. The only variable is time.

Of course, this means that once you've invested money into a lead generation program for three months, the third and fourth months will be much, much more profitable than the first couple months.

Why? *Because you're finally converting all the leads that were generated in previous months.* You're reaping what you sowed. It's harvest time!

Real estate lead generation is not random. It is sequential.

Frustrated agents usually assume that lead generation is random and spontaneous. They think it should work evenly. They ignore the obvious sales cycle. And their short-term perspective limits their risk tolerance!

Failing to see their business in 90-day quarterly cycles, *they inevitably underinvest in lead generation.*

It's like saying October is a more profitable month for farmers than April. Not necessarily...fall harvest is just the natural consequence of planting seeds in the springtime! A farmer would be foolish to give up in the middle of the summer heat before he has the opportunity to reap what he's sowed.

And a real estate agent would be foolish to prematurely give up on a lead generation program just because the leads haven't *yet* converted.

Let's say you invested $5,000 in marketing over 90 days. Did those ads create at least $5,000 of directly attributable income? If so, keep going!

If not, ask yourself one more question: am I currently cultivating any qualified leads that may convert next month? It would be a damn shame to prematurely shut down an advertising campaign that *would have* become incredibly profitable the fourth month.

Don't make this mistake!

In a high value, low frequency industry like real estate, you don't need lots of sales to justify your marketing investments. In most cases, one transaction will pay for multiple months of marketing.

Invest accordingly.

Chapter Fifteen: The Three Metrics That Prove Your Real Estate Marketing Program Is Working (Even Before You Close A Transaction)

With apologies to marathon runners, Olympic athletes, and the brave souls who have climbed Mount Everest, one of the greatest tests of human courage is the first 90 days of a real estate career.

Few endeavors involve the persistence, ambition, and determination of launching a real estate business from scratch. This challenge is repeated when an agent embarks upon a new marketing program.

To be fair, it's hard to get started in any sales career. Sales success, unlike most other professions, is a *direct* function of value creation. In many careers, it is possible to create minimal value yet still achieve moderate levels of external success.

This is because non-value creating activities are great at taking up time, and giving the illusion of hard work. In many jobs, it is fairly easy to "hijack" the value created by other people, and claim it as your own. Most people aimlessly drift through their careers, mistaking activity for actual achievement.

In many companies, no one knows the difference. Nor do they care.

A typical employee can glide through days, weeks, and even months without producing any serious value. *And they will still get paid.*

(If they know how to navigate the office politics, they can even get promoted!)

In most professions, you can attend meetings, organize conference calls, give safe and predictable answers to questions, email incessantly, and cruise through your day feeling "successful."

Because of the size of many organizations, the original source of value creation is concealed. Most people grossly overestimate the few instances in a given year where serious, consequential value is created.

In most businesses, it is a few strategic decisions, breakthroughs, and key sales that create the revenue necessary to sustain the entire annual operation. At the most, this activity represents 5% of the energy expenditure.

The other 95% of time is spent enjoying the "slack" created by the ultra-effective five percent. It looks like work. It might even *feel* like work. But not all work creates value. These terms are not synonymous.

It is possible to put in the time and simply blend in, failing to actually create any valuable business outcomes.

This is not so in real estate. You can't fake progress.

There is no weekly paycheck to numb your ambition. There is no guaranteed income, whatsoever. A real estate agent either creates value, or he will soon find himself in a new career!

It's similar to a tech startup: you can only iterate for so long without a revenue source. Eventually, you have to create real income. Potential is not an asset that shows up on balance sheets.

It does not matter one bit if you are putting in 40 hours a week, or even eighty hours a week. It does not matter if you're prospecting night and day, sending complex direct mail packages to expired listings, or cold calling FSBO's until your voice is hoarse.

As a real estate entrepreneur, you don't get paid for your time. You get paid for the *value* you create. Of course, it takes time to create value for people. But they are not the same thing. Not even close.

Most people coast through their careers, *putting in the time*...but failing to create substantial value. And they wonder why they cannot escape the rat race!

Struggling entrepreneurs blur this distinction. They falsely believe that if they put in more time, things will eventually work out.

But most of the time, things do not work out. Time is not a substitute for value.

When it comes to real estate marketing, creating value means measuring your advertising campaigns. You must hold your marketing dollars accountable. Instead of just running random ads, ask yourself, "Is my advertising creating real value?"

(As evidenced by the fact that it's actually generating viable leads.)

What you need is objectivity. What you need is certainty. What you need is a set of objective metrics that will reveal the effectiveness of your marketing initiatives. Or lack thereof.

The goal is simple: we don't want to prematurely kill off a good marketing program because we *feel* like it's not working.

(Or the inverse, which is probably worse: continuing a poor advertising campaign because we *feel* like it's working.)

If I can narrow down the cause of marketing failure to one thing, it would be *relying on emotions in lieu of data.*

In business, there is no room for feelings. Only facts. You are a real estate entrepreneur, not a corporate bureaucrat. Unlike MBA's working at publicly traded companies, you are spending your own cash. When you make a strategic marketing investment, it's not risking "company money." Your money and the company's money are one and the same.

You do not have the luxury of categorizing failures as "learning experiences."

As a real estate entrepreneur, you must create a direct, causal relationship between your advertisements and your income.

This reality eliminates any possibility of the default decision-making model favored by most small business owners: *doing that which feels good.*

In a high value, low volume business model like real estate, there is no room for warm fuzzies. As Ayn Rand said, "You can avoid reality, but you cannot avoid the consequences of avoiding reality."

And the reality is that it takes time to build a sales funnel! Picking the high hanging fruit isn't easy. If it were, everyone would do it.

The sales cycle inherent in a real estate transaction makes it notoriously difficult to create momentum when first starting out. Inside of 90 days, it's almost impossible to know if what you're doing is working.

Or not working.

This frustration causes most agents to prematurely abandon marketing campaigns *that were working*—they just didn't know it. Worse yet, they didn't know that they could know.

Call it marketing epistemology: it's not what you don't know that hurts you, *it's what you don't think you can know.*

Rephrased as a question: how quickly would your real estate business grow if you knew within 48 hours if an ad campaign was working....and you could pivot accordingly? Cancel ineffective ads, leverage the winners.

Where would your business be three months from now if you could skip the historical 90-day sales cycle?

In advertising, as in life, knowledge is power.

From a professional marketer's perspective, progress depends on making tiny, incremental improvements based on what worked and what didn't work...but traditionally, real estate agents don't get any real feedback until they close (or fail to close) a transaction.

It's an all or nothing proposition: either an ad campaign generates a buyer/seller who in turn generates a commission check, or it doesn't. Binary results.

With this traditional real estate marketing mindset, there are no "checkpoints" to measure the effectiveness of the campaign. There are no mid-funnel metrics, or intermediary goals. Fluffy metrics like Facebook likes or impressions don't pay the bills....*dollars do.*

Either it produced a sale or it didn't. It's black and white. And because it usually takes 60-90 days for a raw lead to be cultivated, there is simply no way of knowing beforehand if a campaign is a dud.

It's an expensive game, no less risky than a weekend of thrills at the casino.

When the feedback loop takes 90 days to provide you with admittedly rudimentary analytics, it turns advertising into little more than a guessing game.

Inside this paradigm, hiring a "professional" marketer is a cruel euphemism. Best case scenario? They are merely better guessers than you are.

Unfortunately, most real estate agents have accepted the 90-day sales cycle as gospel truth. They simply assume that marketing iteration happens in 90-day increments.

And this isn't limited to infamous "top of mind" advertising channels designed to build your brand (think billboards, radio ads, and other mass media). Even with hardcore "direct response" strategies like online pay-per-click advertising or targeted direct mail, it's still difficult to measure the actual ROI of a campaign until it's too late.

Most agents do not have the cash reserves to pump $10,000 (or $1,000, for that matter) into an unknown marketing idea. When the cash register is not ringing, you can only rely on your intuition for so long.

"This will start working, we just need more saturation." Keep telling yourself that! This is what media companies selling you ad space (newspapers, Facebook, the radio station) want you to think.

I call it the *advertising-industrial complex.*

"Eventually you'll reach a critical mass of saturation where your ads become effective," they say.

"Keep advertising, because someone needs to see your message at least 7x for it to sink in," they say.

"Advertising makes you look successful, which makes it more likely people will want to work with you," they say.

Of course, all of these pathetic talking points are *rationalizations.* They are attempting to rationalize why you should keep spending money on something that is not working.

REALITY CHECK: ignorant patience is not a strategy.

However, there are objective ways of measuring an advertising campaign, *even before one of the leads reaches the closing table.*

Three specific metrics, to be exact.

Email open rate, click rate, and engagement.

But before we dive into the details, I have a quick question...

How long can you hold your breath underwater?

I know, it's a strange thing to ask in a book about real estate marketing. Trust me here.

Do you remember what it felt like the last time you dove into a pool?

The first few seconds are an adrenaline rush. You don't really worry that you technically cannot breathe, because you aren't even aware of the oxygen shortage.

However, after a couple seconds, the lack of air becomes an issue—you must swim your way back to the surface. A mild panic sets in. You kick your legs and paddle your arms. Your brain focuses 100% of its conscious energy on doing whatever it takes to get back above the surface of the water where you can breathe.

Even in a backyard pool, where the depth rarely exceeds ten feet, your mind enters a primal state of emergency.

For those couple seconds where you are resurfacing, your brain is in full-blown *survival mode.* It cannot tell the difference between a leisurely pool party and a life-threatening "man overboard" situation on the open ocean.

As you swim closer to the surface, your brain calms down, because you consciously know you're almost there.

But a funny thing happens with your lungs—they don't care. They don't give a damn whether you're ten feet underwater or ten inches underwater.

Why? Because the situation remains unchanged: you still cannot breathe. Regardless of the actual depth, submersion means lack of oxygen. Period. Your brain can sense progress, *but your lungs cannot.* From your lung's perspective, you are either underwater or you're not.

So, who's right—your brain or your lungs?

Does incremental progress matter if you haven't crossed the ultimate finish line?

When it comes to real estate marketing, the answer is a definite *yes.*

The real reason most agents live paycheck to paycheck is because they've failed to put in the necessary mental work of clarifying their marketing goals.

How do you define victory? How do you define a win? And, perhaps more importantly, how would you define failure?

As a real estate entrepreneur, it is imperative to treat marketing not as an art, but as a science. You cannot guess which ads are working or not working. You must form hypotheses, run experiments, control for variables, and act on the results. If you're not willing to do this, hire someone who will do it for you! If you don't, *your competition will.*

Do you have a goal for your CPL (cost per lead) that allows you to objectively compare the effectiveness of different campaigns? Do you have a goal for CPS (cost per sale)? You should know, to the dollar, how much it costs you to produce an actual commission check.

(For most of my Platform™ clients, the CPS goal is 10% of gross commission. So for every $500 we invest into ads, we expect to generate a $5,000 client. For every $1,000 we invest, a $10,000 commission check, etc.)

These are the basic numbers you should be tracking. If you are not tracking these metrics, you don't have a business. You have a *hobby.* And it's increasingly likely that other, more dedicated and ambitious agents will kick your butt.

It's quite simple, really. Three words to transform your business: *know your numbers.*

Of course, knowing your numbers is just the start. To build a lasting real estate business, you must design a responsive marketing plan that gives you instant feedback. The faster you can iterate, the faster you can scale your business!

This is the essence of growth hacking.

Most sales funnels are completely lacking in nuance. They are too simplistic. They are black and white. They don't account for quality, viable leads *that just aren't ready yet.* They don't account for buyers that will be ready to start house hunting in two months when their apartment lease expires, or sellers that plan on selling their house after they've renovated the kitchen.

When you pick the high hanging fruit, these situations are not the exception. They are the rule.

Unless you're buying all of your leads from a search aggregator like Zillow (in which I would argue you are closer to being a Zillow employee than you are an entrepreneur), finding prospects that are ready to take action RIGHT NOW is a rarity.

Whether you realize it or not, your income is usually determined by your conversion rate on these "top funnel" leads.

Everyone can convert a lead that's ready to go, because they are already converted! When a prospect calls you out of the blue and says they're ready to start house-hunting, you didn't "convert" them. When your brother's best friend emails you to let you know he wants you to list his home for sale, you didn't convert him. Anybody with a pulse could "convert" these leads.

The highly skilled, highly specialized (and therefore highly paid) work that most real estate agents struggle to master is true *lead conversion*—knowing how to take a prospect from being casually interested in buying/selling to actually listing their home for sale, or going house-hunting as a buyer client.

This process can take months (although most of it can be automated).

And this is what separates top producers from struggling agents: the size and speed of their lead generation pipeline.

To be blunt, most agents don't have one.

Not everyone has the skill (or patience) to cultivate prospects throughout the sales cycle, and gently nudge them towards the finish line. Anyone can show houses or pound a for sale sign into the front yard; not everyone can navigate the sales cycle that comes before this. Picking the high hanging fruit requires skill!

Many agents don't have a lead generation problem. They have a lead conversion problem. And this starts with a failure to diagnose the prospects already in your pipeline.

Here's the three metrics we monitor for all of our clients: *email open rate, click rate, and engagement.*

By tracking these metrics, we are able to optimize the lead generation funnel and prove it's working....*even before a client buys or sells.*

For example, by monitoring these three metrics, we could launch an ad on February 4th and know by February 6th if the ad is working. Once we've confirmed (or denied) that the ad is producing *quality* leads, we can immediately leverage the campaign. It's not uncommon for my clients to double, or even triple, their ad spend based on this early evidence.

Needless to say, knowing your numbers is the ultimate competitive advantage!

By accelerating the feedback loop, we can iterate faster. We can run more split tests. We can drop the losing ads and leverage the winners.

The only reason you would not keep track of these metrics is if you hate money. And if you're still reading this book, I will assume that is not the case.

Here is a quick breakdown of how to manage the "magic three."

1.) Email Open Rate

This is fairly straightforward.

What percentage of your leads are actually opening your emails?

When we design automated follow up campaigns for Platform™ clients, the metric our team is always trying to optimize is the email open rate.

When a client emails us asking why they haven't converted any leads (yet), the first thing we check is their overall email open rate. Are the new leads they are generating opening the follow up emails?

What is the average open rate of mass emails going out to the entire database?

Our goal is always **25% or higher** (the average real estate agent's open rate is 10-20% at best).

Of course, a 25% open rate means that for every 100 prospects in your database, 25 are actively opening your mass emails.

These mass emails are not disguised as personal emails. The prospect knows it is a mass email being sent to a large list of people. They know it wasn't personal correspondence sent only to them. This amplifies the significance of your email open rate. When people know that they are receiving a mass unpersonalized email, *and they still open it*, it's a great indicator that you're building quantifiable trust with your database.

If you can maintain a 25% email open rate—even to prospects who are fully aware it is a mass email—it is only a matter of time before some of those leads convert!

This is a valuable proxy metric because it measures the quality of your leads *without them knowing you are qualifying them.*

Normally, when you start asking sales questions like "What is your timeline," "Are you already working with a real estate agent," or "What's your budget?", the prospect is fully aware that you are qualifying them.

That's why it's so hard to get quality information from your leads—they don't want to play along. They know the sales game. They know you will follow up with them based on their answers.

So they choose a less intrusive alternative: they dodge the questions.

One of my favorite ways of getting around this is using proxy metrics like email open rate *that the prospect isn't aware we are monitoring.*

Even though we are well into the 21st century, most people are not aware that marketing software allows you to track who is opening your emails. You can even track how many times they open emails. You can track which links they click. This is extremely valuable information when determining the "quality" of your leads.

Monitoring the email open rate is a stealthy way of qualifying leads without them knowing.

Prospects will do just about anything to *avoid detection* as a quality lead. They don't want you to know that they are serious leads! Because as soon as you do, they know you will follow up accordingly.

Keeping track of your email open rate allows you to measure the quality of the leads in your pipeline, even if they aren't responding to your follow up calls or messages. **Usually, this lack of response doesn't mean they are "bad leads." It simply means they aren't far enough along in the sales cycle to feel comfortable talking with a real estate agent.**

If the email open rate is where it should be (25% or higher), you have nothing to worry about. The leads will eventually convert—it's simply a matter of time.

And the reason is simple...

They don't want you to know that they are a serious lead, because they hate the resulting follow up. Their idea of hell is taking phone calls from an overzealous real estate agent. They absolutely do not want to be categorized as a "warm lead" by a real estate agent, even if they plan on buying a home in the near future! They want to operate on their own timeline, and communicate with a real estate agent *only when they are ready.*

Of course, there is no guarantee that this real estate agent will be you. That's why it's our job to connect with them early in the sales cycle to cement the relationship. By providing valuable information and insights, we build trust with them without it feeling like selling. This is the essence of what it means to pick the high hanging fruit!

When the time is right, there won't be an awkward phone call where you attempt to "close the sale." If you provided value early in the sales cycle, the implicit decision to work with you has already been made.

Which brings me to magic metric number two: click rate.

2.) Click Rate

One step beyond the email open rate is the click rate. This is simply the number of times prospects are actually clicking on links in your emails. It proves they are actively engaged with the content you are sending them, regardless of whether or not they are answering your phone calls or manual follow up attempts.

Again, the reason this is so effective is that they are not aware you are monitoring it! Most prospects simply do not know that you can keep track of which links they click. If they are actively engaging with your follow up by clicking links within emails (such as an article on your blog about *4 Strategies For Selling Your Home Quickly In A Slow Market*), you can bet that they are qualified leads!

And this applies beyond email marketing—you should also monitor the click rate on your retargeting ads. If you have strong click rate on retargeting ads (campaigns that only show up to people who have previously visited your website), you have the confidence of knowing that you're attracting quality leads.

(We use retargeting ads for all of our Platform™ clients. It's an incredibly effective strategy for staying "top of mind" during a long sales cycle.)

To maximize the click rate during a typical real estate sales cycle, make sure you're using quality content that provides actual value...not just a sales pitch. Write valuable articles, produce high quality informational videos, and create tools that solve problems for your prospects.

Our clients use a variety of mortgage calculators, multiple-choice quizzes, and other tools to encourage leads to *interact* with their brand (the Platform™ system automates all of this for you).

There is a world of difference between someone that sees your email, and someone who sees your email *and then interacts with the content* by clicking onto your custom mortgage calculator or multiple choice quiz (to "find out if your home could sell in 30 days or less").

In other words, the goal of the email open rate is maximizing the click rate!

Anything you can do to maximize the frequency of these interactions will ultimately result in the holy grail of conversion metrics: engagement.

3.) Engagement

Engagement is the ultimate indicator of a successful marketing campaign. Even if you have not closed a deal from your database of leads, the number of engaged leads will tell you how soon you can expect conversions.

Simply put, I define engagement as *personal communication between you and a prospect.*

After you evaluate the email open rate and click rate of your various campaigns, engagement is the most valuable, qualitative metric to monitor. It's the definitive proof of a successful lead generation campaign.

An advertising campaign could have terrific cost per click and cost per lead, but if none of the leads are actively engaged with you in real conversations (however short), the campaign might not be as successful as you think.

Short of an actual commission check, the number of engaged leads is the best way to measure the success of your marketing strategy.

How many people are having an actual conversation with you?

When a prospect responds to one of your emails, that is engagement. When they answer your phone call and have a short 2-minute conversation with you, that is engagement. When they message you back after you text them, that is engagement. When they respond to your comment on Facebook, that is engagement.

Engagement proves that the prospect is a hot lead, because they have made a conscious decision to communicate with you....*and they understand the consequences of that decision.*

Of course, the "consequence" is simple: you will communicate back. In this sense, they have invited you to be their real estate agent. All you need to do is serve them with integrity, and it's a done deal.

Any time a prospect makes a conscious decision to start a conversation with you (whether by email, text, phone, etc), you must mark them down on a special list. Most real estate CRM's allow you to take notes and "tag" prospects. Whether you use CRM software or an old fashioned legal notepad, make sure to maintain an updated list of everyone who has engaged with you. These are the warmest, highest quality leads.

Even if it's been a while since you've heard back from them, treat these prospects like gold! Anyone willing to communicate with you is worthy of long-term cultivation efforts.

In fact, this is such an important skill, I have dedicated an entire chapter to it!

Keep reading to discover *How To Get Potential Buyers And Sellers To Talk With You...Even If They Hate Real Estate Agents.*

Chapter Sixteen: How To Get Potential Buyers And Sellers To Talk With You...Even If They Hate Real Estate Agents

Have you ever followed up with a lead, only to have them completely ignore your communication?

Of course you have. If you haven't, you're either lying or it's your first week in real estate!

The simple truth is that many prospects will not respond to follow up. At all.

They will completely ignore you. Sure, they may have voluntarily opted-in to download your free e-book, requested information about a listing they saw online, or called you after seeing your number listed on a yard sign. However the connection was created, you managed to get their contact information!

Congrats. You're already farther than most agents, who struggle to attract any leads whatsoever, and therefore resort to cold-calling FSBO's and expired's.

But it means nothing *unless you can create an actual conversation with them.*

This is the real estate equivalent of making fire. The discovery of fire (and the ability to create it) was a game changer for mankind thousands of years ago.

It can be a similar game changer for your real estate career.

I'm going to share two secrets for converting unresponsive leads, but first, we need to get clear on *why leads are unresponsive in the first place.*

Have you ever called a prospect multiple times, only to be greeted by their voicemail message? After a couple times, the pleasant sounding voice almost begins to sound cynical and sarcastic. Perhaps even passive aggressive!

When you've called a prospect four times, you begin to seriously question the integrity of their voicemail message: *Hi, you've reached John Doe. Please leave a short message and I'll get back to you as soon as possible. Thanks, and have a great day.*

To add insult to injury, you can tell that John was smiling when he recorded it. His voicemail greeting sounds cheerful! Why is he giving you the cold shoulder?

Does John really mean it? If he did, wouldn't he have responded by now?

"He must be ignoring me," you think to yourself. "I should just move on to the next lead. No sense wasting more time on John. I don't want to risk angering him, just in case he becomes interested in the future."

When you're emotionally frustrated, this line of thinking seems reasonable. After a couple failed follow up attempts, you don't want to risk annoying John....*just in case he becomes a viable lead in the future.*

It would be foolish to anger him by demonstrating your persistence, right? After all, you don't want to seem desperate. It seems like the rational thing to do. Especially considering that John clearly isn't interested in talking with a real estate agent! If he were, he would have answered the phone, right?

Wrong.

What if John is actually interested *right now*, but you are mistaking a simple sales objection as complete and total rejection?

If you've been making this mistake in your follow up, this changes everything.

After successfully transforming the follow up results of agents all over the country, in both big and small markets, I am convinced that "unresponsive" leads present a massive opportunity. Almost every agent I've met gives up on prospects who don't respond after the first couple follow up attempts. After a few emails or phone calls, the agent gets frustrated and simply surrenders.

This is commonplace, even though we've all seen the statistics that the average sale is made after five or more follow up attempts. Because of the lengthy sales cycle inherent in a real estate transaction, this statistic is *amplified* in the real estate industry. There may be ten or more follow up touches required to convert a lead!

Yet most agents give up after the first couple attempts. Exceptions prove the rule.

(Not surprisingly, the exceptions are the most successful agents. Literally, the *exceptional* agents.)

You are probably well aware that rejection is simply part of the game. Savvy real estate agents quickly learn not to take it personally.

And while it's true that learning to accept rejection is arguably the most important part of a sales career, it's equally true that overcoming objections is the fastest way to accelerate your real estate career.

Don't accept objections....overcome them!

And that's exactly what follow up rejection is: an *objection.* We just call it by a different name when a lead actually starts talking—rejection becomes objection.

Make no mistake, they are the same thing.

Rather than being intimidated by unresponsive leads ("I must be bothering them if they are ignoring my follow up"), think of their lack of communication as a simple *objection.* Nothing more, nothing less.

Most agents have completed some sort of training, however rudimentary, on the basics of overcoming objections. To be frank, it's not rocket science.

Objections aren't scary. They aren't insurmountable. Overcoming objections is table stakes if you want to become a successful real estate agent! It's not "icing on the cake." It's not a skill that's "nice to have. " It is essential.

And it's the price of entry if you want to compete with top agents.

In fact, there has probably never been a real estate transaction, on the buy side or the sell side, where the agent didn't have to overcome at least a few objections.

Maybe your unrealistic seller stubbornly refuses to make a counter on a serious offer from buyer. Maybe your buyer is convinced that interest rates will drop in the future, so they decide to play the waiting game instead of jumping on perfect opportunities.

These are not deal-killers. They're simply objections that need to be overcome.

At its most basic level, overcoming objections is simply *learning to ask better questions.*

Ask any top-producing agent, and they'll tell you that successfully overcoming objections is one of the most important skills, if not THE most important skill, to master. In fact, it's almost impossible to earn a high-income selling real estate without strong sales skills.

Simply put, your income will match your ability to overcome objections. If you are just "average," your income will also be average. If you are excellent, your income will be excellent. It's really that simple.

The ability to overcome objections requires that the agent have a firm belief that every lead is a good lead. *There are no bad leads!* Some leads simply have questions that need to be answered, OR need help re-examining the very questions they're asking.

Regardless, an unresponsive lead is not a "dead" lead or a "bad" lead. There is *not* a lack of communication, even though it may seem that way.

It's actually the opposite: they are communicating loud and clear! They are communicating an implicit objection: they don't think you can help them right now.

If you change their minds, if you *overcome that objection*, you earn the right to have a conversation with them.

To quickly summarize, step one is realizing that an unresponsive lead isn't a bad lead. It simply means they haven't yet decided that you are able to help them. They don't yet believe that you can provide value to them.

It's your job to prove to them that *it's actually in their best interest to communicate with you.* That is the essence of lead conversion.

Of course, it's easier said than done. Lead conversion is a problem for most agents because prospects don't want to talk to them!

In most situations—especially if you are intelligently targeting "top funnel" leads—converting prospects into clients isn't an issue of activating a passive lead with neutral feelings.

That would be an understatement.

Most leads actively and adamantly do not want to talk to you. They aren't merely hard to get a hold of, they *actively resist* your attempts to "convert" them into an appointment.

And I can't blame them! Most follow up is inherently selfish. The only person who benefits from the conversation is the agent! When most real estate agents call/email to follow up with leads, their questions reveal their mentality: they don't want to actually help, they just want to qualify the lead so they don't waste their time.

I get it. There is nothing more frustrating for an agent than spending time on leads who aren't qualified to buy a house, or potential sellers who are just testing the waters.

As a real estate agent, you are routinely abused for information. Sellers contact you for a comprehensive market analysis report, and then turn around and list their home as

For Sale By Owner. Buyers expect you to drive them around on weekends touring homes, and they insult sellers with lowball offers you are embarrassed to present.

Oh, and then you find out they won't even qualify for financing because they exaggerated their income (lied) to the loan officer.

Awesome.

So, really, I get it. I understand why agents are careful about who they work with. I understand why it's necessary to qualify potential clients early on in the process, to avoid the aforementioned nightmare scenarios.

But look at how this feels from the prospect's perspective.

In a world where you never get a second chance to make a first impression, your first impression is providing no value whatsoever.

In fact, quite the opposite. You are attempting to *extract* value from the conversation. There is no trade, just plunder. It is a zero sum game. You win; they lose.

When you open a real estate conversation by asking for additional contact information, or obvious qualifying questions about their income, timeline, or motivation, you send a very clear message: *I'm not interested in helping you until you help me first.*

Only if they "prove themselves" will you consider adding value to the exchange by authentically investing your time and energy.

Until then, most agents want to take, take, take. They forget that it's a two-way street.

First, they need to give, give, give.

And in case you forgot, you need *their business* more than they need *yours*. The supply/demand ratio of real estate agents to clients is incredibly one-sided. There is a far greater supply of agents than the demand warrants. This dynamic decidedly favors the client, not the real estate agent.

From the prospect's perspective (which is the only perspective that matters), there are hundreds of licensed real estate professionals they could choose to work with.

Yet most agents act as if they are entitled to their business! Hmmm....

Should it really be that surprising when prospects seem hesitant or skeptical when we attempt to strike up a conversation?

They know the game you're playing. They know they are just a number to you. So why the hell should they keep playing the game? If you don't have the common decency to first provide value, and *then* subtly ask some "qualifying" questions, why should they waste their time talking to you?

It's like parents asking their kids for presents on Christmas morning. Shouldn't it be the other way around?

Look at the situation from *their* perspective—in most markets, there are hundreds (if not thousands) of licensed real estate agents. Statistically, most of these agents are starving for business at any given time. With the supply and demand ratio firmly in their favor, clients know they can be demanding.

They have high expectations.

The solution is obvious: prove to them that you can solve their problems *by actually solving their problems.* Some people call this "results-based selling." It probably doesn't need a fancy name; it's merely common sense.

Figure out what problems your prospects are having, and solve them. Figure out what information they're looking for, and proactively give it to them.

If you have a list of seller leads, you can probably make some assumptions about their "pain points."

- You know they are wondering *what their home is worth.*
- You know they are wondering *how long it might take to sell.*
- You know they are wondering *what they should do to prepare for listing.*

Now, of course, these are all obvious concerns. And that's the point! There are no secrets in real estate marketing. It really is simple: find out what your prospects want, and make it easy for them to get it.

When you position yourself as a local expert providing valuable information, you are implicitly selling yourself without having to actually "sell." It's frictionless, almost effortless.

And most importantly, it works.

To follow up with seller leads, all you have to do is activate one of the above "pain points," and then provide an immediate solution to the problem.

Let's imagine you are serving the Tucson, Arizona real estate market. You have a list of ten seller leads you acquired that have been completely unresponsive up until this point. You are about to delete them from your CRM and move on, but you decide to send them one last email...just in case.

You could email these seller leads and say:

SUBJECT LINE: Tucson home prices

Hey Bob, I hope you're having a great day. Just wanted to check in— were you still thinking about selling your home this year?

I use variations of this email with almost all of our Platform™ clients. To put it simply, *this follow up template works.* It usually has an email open rate of 40% or higher!

And beyond an amazing open rate, many leads that were previously unresponsive respond to an email like this. They don't just open it. They actually *reply*. They start a conversation with you!

To be honest, these tactics are common sense. Yet I am (consistently) amazed how quickly common sense is abandoned when real estate agents are cultivating leads.

REMEMBER: the only goal of follow up is to get the prospect to respond. That's it. Nothing more. Nothing less.

You won't close a prospect on the initial follow up email, so don't try. You won't be able to qualify them on the initial follow up email, so don't try. You won't be able to establish their timeline, motivation, or credit score on the first email....so don't try!

The real reason most real estate agents fail to convert these leads is because *they are too aggressive.*

Read that again, in case you were unconsciously skimming this section.

In fact, I'm going to repeat it for emphasis: the real reason most agents fail to convert leads is because they are too aggressive.

Almost instinctively, frustrated real estate agents think the cause of their struggles is a *lack of* aggression. They think they need to become even more aggressive. They think they need to increase their sales intensity. They think they need to develop a fearless, killer instinct if they are going to convert more leads.

And so they subject themselves to hours of painful cold calling, using the most aggressive (and cheesy) sales scripts imaginable.

Trust me—if you think it's awkward lying to a FSBO and telling them you "may" have a buyer, it's even more awkward listening to this nonsense. There are more dignified, respectful ways to convert leads.

And lucky for you, taking the high road has another key advantage: it's more effective.

Contrary to what you've been taught in sales seminars, there is a profound difference between an aggressive strategy and an aggressive tactic.

Aggressive *strategies* are great—targeting expired listings, asking for referrals from your existing database, even door knocking a desirable neighborhood. Tactics are *how you actually implement these strategies.*

When it comes to converting leads, you cannot be aggressive on the initial follow up attempts. Any leads who succumb to an early hard-sell are more than outweighed by the majority who do what prospects do best: *simply ignore you.*

So don't try to do too much. While it may seem like a silly metaphor, converting a lead is similar to dating: the only way to have a reasonable chance at a second date is to make the first date a positive experience.

When you immediately start asking intrusive qualifying questions, or worse, simply sending them an application form to fill out, it's the real estate equivalent of popping a marriage proposal on the first date.

It's obnoxious, undignifying, and ultimately, *ineffective.*

This would never work. Besides being incredibly awkward, it's simply not pragmatic! Even if you both had matching compatibility test results, you cannot progress this quickly through the "sales cycle" of a relationship.

Going too far too soon is a surefire way to destroy a relationship before it ever has a chance to develop.

And that's exactly what the prospect wants: a relationship.

It's important not to overlook the fact that when a buyer or seller lead clicks on one of your ads, *they don't know you.* Not only do they not know you, they don't even know what criteria to use when comparing different real estate agents.

Even if they were to interview five or six agents who wanted their business, they would have no idea what questions to ask. They wouldn't even know the criteria to compare them on.

They are completely ignorant when it comes to knowing what characteristics to look for in a real estate agent—*and they know it.*

They know what they don't know. And so the question of whom to work with isn't easily answered by how many homes you've sold this year, or how many years you've been in the business. You can brag about these "impressive" statistics, but it won't impress them.

Ultimately, the decision isn't as logical as it is emotional. In their minds, the only relevant question is...do they trust you? They are not going to trust the largest financial transaction of their life to someone they don't...*trust.*

Are you sensing a pattern here?

It's all about trust. The faster you build trust, the faster you will convert leads. It's that simple.

"Lead conversion" is simply a euphemism for *trust building.*

How would your mindset about lead generation change if you started referring to it as *trust building?*

"Wow, I had a great day at the office! I earned the trust of 3 prospects. I have a total of fifty leads in my funnel, so that's a 6% trust percentage! If only I could build trust with a few more, I would be practically printing money!"

Every time you catch yourself saying the phrase "lead conversion," consider substituting the phrase *trust building.* It will transform your mindset, and thus transform your results.

And that brings up an interesting question: what is the most effective way to build trust?

Well, I'm glad you asked! By far, an *authentic conversation* is the fastest way to accelerate the trust building process. Yes, it's helpful if the prospect reads your emails. Yes, it's helpful if the prospect reads your blog posts. Yes, it's helpful if the prospect watches some of your videos on YouTube. Yes, it's helpful when the prospect sees your posts on social media.

All of the above work together to create a cumulative effect of *familiarity* (a powerful marketing concept from Robert Cialdini's book *Influence*).

In a nutshell, the principle of familiarity states that any contact, whatsoever, between your brand and your target consumer is generally a good thing. People grow fond of what is familiar to them.

It's rooted in evolutionary biology. Humans are wired to resist change. We have a vested interested in preserving the status quo. New = dangerous. Unknown = risky. So the more exposure we have to someone or something, the more we begin to subconsciously trust it. *Even if we have no actual evidence to suggest that it's trustworthy.*

According to the familiarity principle, something that is familiar is automatically good.

Now, of course, if you're reading this book, I'm going to assume you are a trustworthy real estate agent with a reputation of integrity. That being said, we'll skip the obvious ethics lecture that typically accompanies Cialdini's Principle of Familiarity.

Here's how this directly applies to real estate marketing: any contact or experience with your brand is a good thing. This is why email follow up, retargeting ads, and testimonials are so important. They keep you top of mind throughout a sometimes-lengthy sales cycle.

But compared to the magical power of an *actual conversation,* nothing even comes close. Staying "top of mind" is pointless unless it leads to authentic conversations. In fact, I would go so far to say that the entire purpose of these initial "touches" (blog posts, social media, etc) is simply priming the prospect.

The goal of these supporting initiatives isn't to convert leads, it's to maximize the likelihood that when you attempt to spark an actual conversation, they are willing to reciprocate.

And that brings me to what might be the most practical advice in this entire book...

The only—and I repeat ONLY—purpose of the first email is to get the prospect to respond.

If they hit "reply" and send a message back to you, *you won.* It's a victory. You successfully convinced them to do something instead of nothing. It's the infinite difference between zero and one. A lead that actually engages with you is qualitatively different from other leads, regardless of whether or not they are merely opening your emails.

Something magical happens when a prospect responds...*trust.*

In the decisive moment a prospect decides to open your email (an outcome you shouldn't take for granted, as over half of all "marketing" emails never get opened), the last thing they want to do is surrender their financial history, buying or selling motivation, and timeline.

They don't even know you!

The first couple back-n-forth emails are about one thing, and one thing only: building trust. Obviously, you cannot build trust if they are ignoring your emails!

And so the burden of proof is on you to compose an irresistible message—*an email that ends with a direct question that cannot be ignored.*

When I say "irresistible," I mean it in the literal sense of the term: the prospect is unable to resist replying.

The perfect follow up email is short, sweet, and right to the point. It has two defining characteristics that make it effective: personalization and expectation.

The first and most important follow up technique is personalization. It must feel personal, *like you manually sat down at your laptop and sent them an individual email.* If they suspect that it was an automatically generated drip email, they will ignore it. Worse, they will ignore all future emails and follow up!

When it comes to lead conversion (trust building), first impression is everything.

Prove to them that you're a real human being by writing the email in such a way that seems personal. The goal is for them to believe that you took the time out of your day to personally send them a follow up message.

This leverages a timeless principle of psychology, the idea of reciprocity. First popularized in Cialdini's book *Influence* (a must-read for any student of marketing) reciprocity is the idea that no one wants to feel like a "moocher." If someone buys you lunch, you offer to pick up the tab next time. If someone opens the door for you, you say thank you. If your friends help you move in to your new house, you volunteer to help them the next time they need help with a household project.

When someone does something nice for us, we want to even the score!

The principle of reciprocity is why personal-sounding emails usually get answered. *If someone took the time to send us an email, we feel like we owe them the courtesy of a response.*

Of course, this has massive implications for real estate marketing. For whatever reason, there is an implicit social contract between human beings where ignoring personal correspondence is considered rude. In other words, if you take the time out of your day to write someone a message, most people will feel compelled to respond....*even if they don't want to.*

Why? Because it would be rude to withhold the basic courtesy of a response. This is why many parties and get-togethers require RSVP's, even when someone will not be attending!

Have you ever considered how strange it is that our culture thinks the burden of action is on the invitee, not the host? If you are unable to attend a party, you are typically expected to notify the host and let them know.

The same can be true of your email marketing, if you leverage the principle of reciprocity when following up with leads.

It all comes down to one word: *expectation.*

Is it clear in your follow up emails that you are *expecting* a response?

The easiest way to achieve "expectation" is to simply make it a habit of always ending your follow up with a short, direct question.

Here are a few examples:

Were you thinking about buying a home this year, or are you just doing some research?

What price range are you looking in?

Have you seen the February market update video?

Do you currently own a home, or are you renting?

Would you like me to give you access to the official database of active listings so you can search for homes on your own?

If you don't mind me asking, how'd you hear about us?

How long have you lived here in Tulsa?

Advertisers have known for decades that your "call to action" should be extremely specific. There should never be any ambiguity in your advertisements. Professional marketing firms and advertising agencies have known this since the early 1900's (Claude Hopkins popularized it in his 1923 book *Scientific Advertising*).

If interested prospects don't know what you want them to do next, they will take the path of least resistance: *they will do nothing.*

The unfortunate reality is that most real estate marketing emails make it very, very easy for the prospect to do nothing. When you don't conclude your email with a direct question, the prospect doesn't feel compelled to respond.

If there is no question that needs to be answered, the prospect would have to go out of his way to type a reply. In other words, you've all but eliminated the possibility of a meaningful conversation.

When there is no expectation of an answer, it's psychologically easy for the lead to delete the email.

"Hmmmm," they think to themselves, "He seems friendly I suppose, but I don't feel ready to start talking with a real estate agent yet." And so they don't.

They delete the email, and forget about it.

Your job is to make sure this never happens again!

Make your emails *irresistible*, in the literal sense of the term: impossible to resist.

It is your responsibility to create a clear expectation in your follow up. When the prospect opens your email, is it clear what you expect them to do next?

As I said, the best way to do this is to ask a direct question. A question that is so clearly worded, *it is obvious that you are expecting a response.*

Ironically, this the opposite of what most real estate agents do. They blabber on and on about fluffy details. They brag about their brokerage, how many homes they sold last year, and other irrelevant statistics. Most follow up emails are several paragraphs long. Some include obviously "template" content like *10 Tips To Maximize Your Home's Value*, or *4 Tips For First-Time Homebuyers.*

Do you think the people reading these emails are morons?

Do you think they actually believe that you sat down at your laptop, and typed 500 words about "10 Tips To Maximize Your Home's Value"....just for them?

No. Of course not.

Obviously, this is a dead giveaway that they are receiving an automatically generated drip email. And the second they realize it's an autoresponder, you can kiss any chance of a conversation goodbye.

FACT: barely anyone reads autoresponder emails....and *no one* replies to them.

That's what doesn't work. And it's probably what you've been doing up until this point!

Here's what *does* work: minimalism. If you keep your initial follow up email to three sentences or less, you will drastically increase the likelihood that leads not only read your email, but actually respond to it.

Long emails trigger the prospect's "bullshit radar." When they receive an email that's more than a couple sentences, they assume it was probably an autoresponder drip email. Most humans do not type three-paragraph emails to total strangers.

It's the online equivalent of a "form letter."

Read through your current autoresponder follow up emails. Do they sound like automatically generated emails?

If so, your email open rate will be less-than-awesome. And worse yet, your engagement rate will be a big fat *zero*.

(Engagement rate is the number of people who not only open your emails, but actually respond to them and start a conversation.)

Keep it simple!

The most effective emails are usually 2-3 sentences long, because that's *believable.* When an email is short, sweet, and to the point, the prospect will believe that you actually sat down and personally wrote it just to them.

Hey Bob, I just saw that you requested some more info about my listing at 145 Oak Ridge Drive. I've attached some photos for you to look over.

Are you thinking about buying a home this year, or are you just doing some research?
-Heather

To create engagement, end your emails with a direct question that implies you're expecting a response. The last sentence is what will create an "open loop" in Bob's mind.

It creates psychological tension.

The only way to resolve that tension is to "close the loop" by responding to your question.

He knows you asked him a direct question, *and it would be rude not to respond.* More than likely, he will say something vague like, "Yes, I'm thinking about it. Just doing research right now, thanks."

And that's all you need.

Now that Bob has responded, you are officially in a *conversation.* You can reply with another direct question to keep the conversation going.

The last sentence (the question) is important to create conversations, but the first sentence sets it all up.

Unfortunately, the opening sentences of most real estate emails are bad. Not just bad. Horrifyingly bad.

But that's good news for you! It means the bar is set very low. If you put just a little thought into crafting your follow up emails, you will build trust with more leads than you ever thought was possible. Remember, build trust = convert!

Here's the game plan:

The opening line is your hook. It's what gets the prospect to open up your email and read the rest. Most email programs (like Gmail) allow you to read the opening sentence or two of an email *before you even open it.* This is called the pre-header text.

Most people completely ignore this when writing emails! And that's a huge mistake. Yes, the subject line is incredibly important. Duh. It's the "ad for the ad." Legendary copywriters have made fortunes on the strength of their headlines alone. I'm not downplaying the importance of a strong email subject line.

But the opening sentence, "the pre-header text," is just as important.

This opening sentence is a huge opportunity to prove that you're a real human being. If that opening sentence sounds too formal or general, it's a dead giveaway that it's an autoresponder drip email.

However, if you open the email with personal words like "I," and reference an action that the prospect just took, it looks and feels personal. The prospect will open the email, and they will be pleasantly surprised that you took the time to send them a personal email.

Here are a few examples of effective opening sentences for your emails:

Hey Bob, I just saw that you signed up for a free copy of my book.

Hey Bob, I just saw that you requested more info about 2457 Skyline Drive.

Hey Bob, I just noticed you requested a free home value report.

When your email starts with a variation of, "Hey Bob, I *just saw* _____," it implies that you literally just noticed the action Bob took, and you quickly sat down at your computer to type out a response.

When Bob reads that, he will visualize you hurriedly grabbing your laptop. Bob will feel special, because you are proving that he's important to you.

This is an incredibly effective way to open an email!

So here's the executive summary: to create maximum engagement with your leads, open your emails with a sentence that sounds like you are personally responding, and end with a direct question.

If you sound like a real human being, you will accelerate the trust building process with your leads. A shorter sales cycle makes everyone happier!

BONUS Chapter: How To Build A Long-Term Business By Picking The High Hanging Fruit
+ some thoughts on the importance of innovation for real estate agents

One of our core values at Platform™ is innovation.

And so we run a lot of experimental ads for our clients. And when I say *experimental ads*, that's a euphemism for "we have absolutely no clue if it's going to work."

Sometimes these ads work. Most of the time they don't. But we aren't aiming for perfection. We're aiming for progress.

In an industry like real estate, even the tiniest of advantages can result in big financial rewards. If a client spends a hundred dollars on a new ad that doesn't work, *who cares.* In fact, let me take that one step further: our most successful clients will spend $1,000 on experimental ads. *And they don't care if they don't work.*

There is no clear ROI on research & development. That's good news, not bad news!

You can't make estimates and projections on the annual profitability of innovation—and that's entirely the point.

What's the ROI of survival? It's a silly question to ask! As the world becomes more and more digital, agents who are not innovative will simply be left behind.

And to avoid any confusion, let me be very clear on what I mean when I say "innovation." I'll be the first to admit it's an overused corporate buzzword! Maybe *the* most overused corporate buzzword.

To some people, innovation might mean launching a Facebook page. To others, it might be a newly designed website. For most real estate agents, the word *innovation* is simply a synonym for technology.

I am not using the term in that sense.

When I say *innovation*, I am referring to something very specific: creating new ads and split-testing them against your existing ads.

In this sense, an ongoing commitment to innovation is an ongoing commitment to continuous profitability.

It's not sexy. The reality is that it's incredibly boring work! Running continuous split-tests is not as interesting as launching a new logo or a fancy website. When most people say they "enjoy" marketing, what they are really saying is they enjoy coming up with ideas, logos, slogans, etc.

In my opinion, that is not marketing.

As you know, there are hundreds of pathetic sounding real estate slogans. None of them generate any business. They are just "cute."

Unfortunately, *cute* doesn't pay the bills:

-From A to Z, contact Dee!
-Call Bill and start packing!
-I hold the "key" to your real estate needs!
-Your referral is the best compliment I can earn!

-Never too busy for your referrals!

-Everything I touch turns to SOLD!

    And this is why marketers are usually viewed with skepticism from the more "sophisticated" business divisions like accounting, finance, or technology.

    The art of real estate marketing can be fun, but the *science* of real estate marketing is where you make all the money.

    As a real estate agent, you must commit to marketing innovation. You must commit to continuous testing. You must commit to treating marketing not as subjective art, but as objective science. Or....hire a marketing firm who will! Our most successful clients (measured by the number of homes they sell every year directly from Platform™ ads) are the same clients who enthusiastically try out new ideas. In some cases, these clients spend more money each year on new "experimental ads" than some real estate agents spend on their total annual marketing budget.

    In this way, real estate marketing is like venture capital. People forget your strikeouts as long as you hit a homerun every now and then. Or, even better, a grand slam.

    We try a lot of new ads, because we don't just want to stay "ahead of the curve." We want to be inventing the curve.

    To be the leader in their markets, our clients have to be willing to take smart risks. The reality is that most new ads don't work.

However, as soon as we discover a new ad concept that *does* work, we can leverage accordingly. If each commission produces $5,000+ of income for our clients, it doesn't take very many "wins" to make up for a lot of temporary losses.

In the world of online marketing, coming up with a "new idea" every 6 months is unacceptable. The world moves much, much faster than that. What worked 6 months ago probably doesn't work today. At all.

That's why ambitious agents hire us to optimize their marketing for them. We spend all day studying, split-testing, and scheming how to stay ahead of the "trends."

And, in many cases, we create the trends.

We're constantly trying new things. Testing new images, new headlines, new demographics to target, entirely new funnel concepts and landing page designs.

If a real estate agent is even *moderately successful*, they simply don't have time for this. They don't fix their own toilet—they hire a professional plumber. They don't file their own taxes—they hire a full-time accountant. They don't do their own oil changes—they get the car serviced by a licensed mechanic. You get the picture.

For ambitious agents, the same is true of their marketing: they trust it to someone who can (literally) spend all day testing, tweaking, and optimizing lead generation.

This is probably the fastest way to accelerate your real estate business—stop trying to do everything yourself, and invest in hiring professionals to do what *they* do best so you can focus on what *you* do best (selling houses).

Here's an interesting thought experiment...

Which of these two scenarios do you think will achieve maximum results in minimum time? Be honest.

1. A stressed-out real estate agent *who is already working 60 hours a week* struggling to figure out the basics of social media ads, split-testing, retargeting pixels, and landing page conversion,

OR

2. A digital marketing professional *who specializes in real estate advertising* and literally spends all day, every day optimizing ad campaigns?

Here's an even better question: which of these two scenarios do you think will create amazing results *the fastest?* Obviously, you will get better results working with an expert! Time is money.

Here at Platform™, if we can average one large-scale "experimental" split test every week, it might not make a huge difference in the short term. But over the course of a year, that's 50 unique experiments! Each experiment has the potential to be a *game-changer* for our clients.

For example, just last week a new split-test (using a slightly different headline and image than we were previously using) resulted in a client's cost-per-lead being cut by over SIXTY PERCENT.

They were previously generating leads with full contact information (including phone number) for about ten bucks. After this split-test, they are now generating those same leads for just three dollars apiece!

That means for the same amount of money they were previously spending, they can generate 3x the leads!

If this were the only "optimization" we made all year to this client's account, it would be a fantastic year. Cutting your marketing costs by 60% is no small feat! This isn't just an "improvement." It's a *game-changer*.

And this insight came from just one-split test. Imagine where your business could (and should be) a year from now, after running dozens of split-tests with your advertising!

This is why successful agents hire companies like Platform™ to maximize their lead generation. We apply the scientific method to real estate marketing: we create hypotheses about why we believe a certain ad will attract buyers/sellers, and then we set out to prove or disprove its validity.

To be completely honest, it can be pretty frustrating! If I had to guess, I'd say we are wrong a solid 80% of the time. 4/5 of our experiments are total failures, where we see no meaningful improvement.

But the other 20% creates such phenomenal results that we quickly forget about the "failed" experiments.

(When you commit to a *culture* of continuous testing and improvement, there's really no such thing as a "failed" experiment. There's either a hypothesis that was proven or disproven. It's a wonderfully liberating mindset.)

Part of the reason Platform™ is so valuable to our clients is that our marketing funnels are designed to cultivate *engagement*, not just a name/email lead. The goal is always to spark a real conversation, by incentivizing the prospect to interact with our clients.

For example, we use a variety of multiple choice quizzes, mortgage calculators, home value calculators, etc. In the very act of "opting in" on a landing page, the prospect is instantly receiving value.

This makes it much more likely that they will engage with the real estate agent. Names and emails are great, but *conversations* are even better!

When we create new ad campaigns for our clients, this is the standard we hold ourselves to: will this new ad create high quality leads that lead to conversations?

If the answer is "no," we keep testing until the answer is *yes*.

That's why I have a big 24x36 framed photo of Ted Williams in my office. It helps me to keep focused on the big picture, and stay optimistic in the midst of "failure."

(Ted Williams is arguably the greatest baseball player of all time. He is the only player to ever bat higher than .400 for an entire season, a feat he accomplished in 1941. This means that the greatest hitter of all time still failed 60% of the time.)

It should be obvious by now that picking the high hanging fruit requires *patience*. It's smart work, not hard work. Building a reliable pipeline of future business takes time! There is no way around this fact.

Because most agents don't have the vision or patience to execute this contrarian strategy, it will remain a competitive advantage for years to come.

Conclusion: The Most Important Question In Real Estate Marketing

So, where should you start?

After reading this book, what's next? Should you launch a new website that's focused on local content? Or should you start writing some actual blog articles, so your new website has valuable content before it goes live?

Do you even need a new website? Maybe you should just spend your time and money on generating more leads.

Of course, quantity without quality is not a viable long-term strategy. Should you invest in a more professional video camera for filming your listing tours and market update videos? Maybe some high-quality wireless microphones?

Hmmm....

There dozens of ways you can take action and start picking the high hanging fruit.

Here's my advice: don't worry about specific tactics until you've solidified your overall marketing strategy. Very, very rarely will *buying stuff* solve your marketing problems.

Marketing results are created by marketing strategies. Sure, having the right tools makes implementing certain strategies easier, but the tools themselves do not guarantee success. It's the wizard, not the wand.

Many real estate professionals (especially those who are already fairly successful and thus have money to burn) think they can just buy their way to growth.

This will not work.

You can invest in the most expensive video production equipment, professional mics, a brand new laptop, and a fancy $5,000 website, but it won't matter if there's not a specific marketing strategy tying it all together. Many of my Platform™ clients got started with nothing more than an iPhone and a basic blog website that cost them less than $1,000 to launch. You'd be surprised how clear the video footage is from a smartphone!

The lesson is clear: don't let perfectionism prevent you from taking action on IMPLEMENTING your marketing strategy.

After reading this book, you've probably created an unofficial mental checklist of half a dozen ideas you'd like to implement.

Here's my advice: just do it. Don't fall into analysis paralysis, trying to prioritize what's the first, second, or third thing you should try. Try them all, all at once. Massive, simultaneous action always beats reflective contemplation.

This is why entrepreneurial startups so often surprise larger, more established competition: they simply take more action.

So don't procrastinate by "buying stuff." You really don't need a brand new video camera, microphones, or a fancy website.

This is the most common *avoidance behavior* I see with new clients. They delay taking action because they need to get the "right stuff."

What's really happening is they're scared of taking action. They're scared of trying something new. They're scared of looking stupid if it doesn't work right away. To disguise their fear of failure, they buy stuff!

"I'll starting creating more videos once I get my new camera."

"I'll start writing more market update reports once I have a new blog."

It's all bullshit. Take Nike's advice and *just do it.*

Waiting until you're "ready" is a more advanced, sophisticated form of procrastination....but it is still procrastination!

You don't need stuff. You need strategies. Once you have the strategies (which you should after reading this book), you only need one more thing: implementation.

That's it. Nothing more, nothing less. Just take action!

To pick the high hanging fruit, you only need a couple important items: a ladder, a basket, and maybe some gloves. No need to complicate things with fancy tools!

The same is true of real estate marketing. The checklist of bare essentials is short. If you already own a laptop and a phone that records video, you're all set. You don't need any more "stuff."

It's difficult to give up the illusion of control in your business. *Especially when things are already going fairly well.* When you try new things, there's always a possibility that they won't work. That's okay. Accept it.

Take action. Don't worry about the details. Real world experience has a funny way of answering all of our unanswered questions...but it's impossible to gather this feedback outside the context of *doing.*

Thinking about a marketing idea will not reduce its risk or amplify its reward. You can only move forward by....actually moving forward.

Here is the simplest action formula for picking the high hanging fruit in your real estate market: *be better at marketing than other real estate agents, and creatively communicate that fact in your own marketing.*

There are two steps to this:

1.) Be better at marketing than the competition
2.) Make sure people are aware of step number one

That's it.

The real reason many agents are unable to pick the high hanging fruit (and instead buy expensive leads from companies like Zillow) is they ignore step number one.

By ignoring step number one, you automatically fail step number two! After all, you can't communicate something that isn't true.

If you aren't *objectively* better than the competition, your marketing messaging will always seem awkward.

This is the predicament most agents find themselves in: they don't know what to say in their advertisements, because *they have nothing interesting to say.*

This is why almost all real estate advertising is boring, uninspiring, and therefore doesn't work. It provides no value to the consumer. When there is no value, there is no reason to respond. And when the consumer has no logical reason to respond to an ad....they will not respond to the ad.

This is not rocket science.

No potential prospect will pick up the phone and call you because you have a fancy logo or a nice smile in your ad. When a buyer or seller takes a risk by contacting you, they are doing so because of *what's in it for them.*

It's not about you, it's about them!

Once you understand this fundamental marketing truth, it should become perfectly obvious that the fastest way to improve your marketing results is to make the decision to contact you a no-brainer. Offer so much value to potential buyers and sellers that *not* responding to your ad feels painful.

Imagine if you saw a newspaper ad for a local bank that said, "FREE MONEY! STOP BY AND CLAIM YOUR FREE $100 BILL. LIMITED TO ONE PER CUSTOMER."

Responding to most ads is emotionally painful. We don't *enjoy* calling the cable company to setup a new account. We don't *enjoy* going to the car dealership to test drive new vehicles. We merely tolerate these interactions because they are a means to an end.

If we could skip talking to the cable company or the car salesman, we would. But we can't. We don't want to befriend the car salesman...*we just want the damn car!* We're forced to endure these interactions to get what we really want.

Contacting a real estate agent is no different. No one *wants to* work with a real estate agent. If they could buy or sell a home without a licensed agent, they would!

As a real estate professional, you are a necessary evil. Your job as a marketer is to make this process as painless as possible. Do not underestimate the emotional inertia of your potential prospects...they do *not* want to contact you.

Your job is to offer them something that's so valuable, they simply cannot resist.

The default reaction to seeing an advertisement is....*drumroll*.....nothing. Most people simply ignore 99% of ads. They don't remember them, and they certainly don't engage with them!

To conceptualize what constitutes a truly "irresistible" ad, it might help to examine the logical extremes. Let's return to the previous example of a local bank giving away hundred dollar bills.

If a local bank were literally giving out free money, you would feel dumber not taking action than you would taking action. Ignoring the ad would cost you a free $100! It's a no brainer.

To successfully pick the high hanging fruit, your real estate advertising must be irresistible to your ideal prospects.

It might not be interesting to everyone, but for the right person, it should be *irresistible.* Anyone who sees your ad that is actually interested in buying/selling a home in the near future should be captivated by your offer. If it doesn't excite them, the ad will not work!

The goal of advertising is not to simply remind potential prospects that you exist. It's not enough to have "top of mind awareness." Good advertising produces actual results, which is to say, good advertising produces *leads.*

The only way to produce leads is to offer something incredibly, incredibly valuable.

In other words, you don't get to pick the high hanging fruit. It picks *you.*

Going after the high hanging fruit is simply a creative way of saying, "offer so much value to others that they are naturally drawn to you."

Ultimately, everything comes down to providing value to the potential prospect. The best way of doing that is *being* valuable. Be a better real estate agent than the competition. Be better at marketing your listings. Be better at finding the perfect home for your buyers.

When you are *objectively* better than the competition, communicating that fact is surprisingly simple. This is the essence of great real estate marketing.

Make sure you have a damn good answer to this question: why should prospects work with YOU, and not your competition?

Do you have a unique, compelling answer to this question?

All of the marketing strategies, tactics, and techniques in this book are simply creative answers to this question.

Picking the high hanging fruit takes more talent, more work, and more brains. It's not a strategy for the faint of heart. To be clear, it won't be easy. Most things in life worth doing aren't!

When you commit to picking the high hanging fruit, you are volunteering to compete in a meritocracy, and perhaps more importantly, you are forcing your competitors to do the same.

So, ask yourself, *why should clients work with YOU, and not your competition?*

As soon as you have a unique and compelling answer to this question, the high hanging fruit will be ripe for the picking.

RECOMMENDED READING

Growth Hacker Marketing
by Ryan Holiday

80/20 Sales and Marketing
by Perry Marshall

Influence
by Robert Cialdini

Scientific Advertising
by Claude Hopkins

Made in the USA
Coppell, TX
25 May 2020

26457959R00105